THE ACTS OF ST. SEBASTIAN

ST. AMBROSE
Archbishop of Milan

Translated by: *D.P. Curtin*

THE ACTS OF ST. SEBASTIAN

Copyright @ 2016 Dalcassian Press

All rights reserved. No part of this publication may be reproduced, distributed, or transmitted in any form or by any means, including photocopying, recording, or other electronic or mechanical methods, without the prior written permission of the publisher, except in the case of brief quotations embodied in critical reviews and certain other non-commercial uses permitted by copyright law. For permission request, write to Dalcassian Press at dalcassianpublishing at gmail.com

ISBN: 979-8-3303-7304-8 (Paperback)

Library of Congress Control Number:
Author: Curtin, D.P. (1985-)

Printed by Ingram Content Group, 1 Ingram Blvd, La Vergne, Tennessee

First printing edition 2016.

THE ACTS OF ST. SEBASTIAN

CHAPTER I. St. Sebastian Encourages the Martyrs.

1. Sebastian, a most Christian man, educated in the parts of Milan, was indeed a citizen of Narbonne, so dear to the emperors Diocletian and Maximian that they entrusted him with the command of the first cohort and commanded him to always stand in their presence. For he was a man of complete wisdom, truthful in speech, just in judgment, prudent in counsel, faithful in what was entrusted to him, vigorous in intervention, conspicuous in goodness, and renowned in the overall integrity of his character. The soldiers revered him as if he were their father; all those in charge of the palace cherished him with the dearest affection: for he was a true worshiper of God, and it was necessary that he, whom God's grace had filled, be loved by all.

2. Therefore, he daily performed diligent service to Christ, but he acted in such a way that it remained hidden from the sacrilegious kings, not terrified by the fear of suffering, nor constrained by the love of his inheritance, but under the cloak of earthly authority he acted as a hidden soldier of Christ, to strengthen the spirits of Christians whom he saw failing amidst tortures, and to return to God the souls which the devil sought to take away.

3. Finally, after he had snatched many minds of martyrs from the fear of suffering and incited them to the crown of everlasting glory: he made himself known, for a light cannot hide in darkness. Therefore, he daily provided consolation to the most illustrious men Marcellian and Marcus, two twin brothers, who were imprisoned for the name of Christ; and he ministered to both them and also their servants, with whom they had been captured, providing them with saving counsel of faith: so that they might reject the fleeting allurements of the world and not fear the momentary kinds of tortures.

CHAPTER II. The Firmness of Marcellian and Marcus is Seriously Attacked.
4. As they acquiesced in the most blessed consolations and endured the scourges of the executioners with a persevering spirit, they were ordered to undergo the death sentence: with the condition that if at the same moment they consented to sacrifice, they would be returned to their parents, wives, sons, and possessions. For they were not only, as we said, of the most noble lineage, but also wealthy; their father was named Tranquillinus, and their mother was called Marcia; who followed them with their wives and children; for they were led by excessive affection for their grandchildren. Hence it happened that they obtained a thirty-day truce from Agrestius Chromatius, the prefect of the city of Rome, during which time negotiations would be conducted with them, so that they might consent to worship idols.

5. Therefore, as their friends approached them, they began to say: Where do you find such a hard mind, such an iron heart, that you cast off the old age of your father, and bring new pains of childbirth upon your already decrepit mother? For she overcame the pains of childbirth with consolations, while in one pain she bore two sons, and poured forth a double affection of sons to her father: but now there is an incurable pain, an inconsolable penalty, an irremediable torment, an incomparable childbirth, by which hope and joy are taken away, life is despised, glory is rejected, and, disregarding all feelings of piety, the cruelty of death is sought rather than feared. We beseech you, O dearest friends, finally put an end to these calamities, and remember that you are the fathers of sweet sons, even if admonished.

6. While the mother was saying these and similar things, crying out in misery, she came, and showing the gray hairs of her old age with her head uncovered, in their sight she tore the garment that covered her breast: and, weeping, she showed them the loose skins that had suckled them, and lamenting, she recalled the comforts she had given them in their infancy. Therefore, she said to both: You have always flattered me more, my son; and you have been more modest: in this one I bore my image, in you I poured forth the features of your father; you are more useful to your father, he is more similar. Woe is me! I am surrounded on all sides by incomparable sorrows, unheard-of misery and double bereavement, which cannot be compared to any tribulations at all. I omit the sons hastening to death of their own accord, whom if enemies were to take away from me, I would follow through the midst of the ranks of soldiers; if violent judgments were to conclude, I would break into prison, dying. This is a new kind of perishing, in which the executioner is asked to strike, life is desired to perish, death is invited to come. This is a new grief; a new misery, in which the youth of my children is willingly lost, and the wretched old age of parents is compelled to live.

7. As the mother continued with such and similar lamentations, the weak father, now heavy with old age, was brought by the hands of servants, and scattering dust on his swan-like head, he raised such voices to heaven: I have come to bid farewell to my sons who are going forth to death, so that I may expend all that I had prepared for their burial. O sons, my staff of old age, and the light of my double entrails, born happily and raised prosperously, of most excellent memory, and of singular talent, imbued with all the knowledge of liberal arts, what sudden madness born from your will has made you lovers of death? Never did this please the living: never did it induce its love in the dying: for whoever could reach it, it was violently imposed, and it was not willingly accepted by any living person. If this naked debtor suffers under a greedy moneylender, he can love in no way; nor is he known to love, but to fear. By what reason does he desire it, who is overflowing with all goods, and owes nothing at all? Come here, old men, and weep with me over the sons who feel that you have paternal entrails. Come here, young men, and weep over the young men who are perishing voluntarily. Come here, fathers, and prevent such things, lest you allow such things to happen. Fail in weeping, O my eyes, and cover the darkness by pouring forth rivers of tears; lest I see those being slain by the sword, whom I trembled at while a light rod touched them; when I saw them faintly sad, I was terrified.

8. Therefore, while the elder was discussing these and other matters, behold, the spouses of both come with their own children, and offering their own infants to their gaze, they pour forth these lamenting voices: To whom do you leave us to serve? To whom do you entrust the love of our marriage? Who do you think will be the masters of these children, and the most eager invaders of your homes? Who will be the occupiers of your family? Or who will divide among themselves the slaves you have nurtured? Alas, how harshly, alas, with what

impious cruelty do you despise your parents, reject your friends, cast aside your wives, abdicate your children, and present yourselves as willing executioners!

CHAPTER III. St. Sebastian strengthens the wavering.

9. Meanwhile, while these things are said, and those are reported, amidst the tears of wives and the sighs of children, the soldiers of Christ began to soften and bend their spirits towards sorrow. St. Sebastian, a most Christian man, who was concealed by military attire and overshadowed by the cloak, was present at this spectacle, as we mentioned above. But when he saw the athletes of God fatigued by the immense weight of the contest, he threw himself in the midst of them and said: O most valiant soldiers of Christ, O most skilled warriors of the divine battle, through excessive strength of spirit you have bravely attained the palm, and now do you lay down the eternal crown through miserable flattery? Let the fortitude of Christ's soldiers be learned through you, to be armed more by faith than by steel. Do not cast aside the insignia of your victories through the flattery of women, and do not loosen the conquered necks of the enemy, laid at your feet, to victorious and revived battles, whose fierce and unjust insistence has been against you, but whose anger is made more savage by repetition. Therefore, raise up a glorious trophy of your contest from earthly affections, and do not lose it to the weeping of little ones.

10. Those whom you see weeping would rejoice today if they could know what you know; for they think that this life is the only one, which, if it comes to an end, no vital soul can remain after the body has perished. For if they knew that there is another life ignorant of death, unaware of sorrow, in which immortality reigns, and eternal joys abide; surely, they would hasten to reach it with you, and counting this life as nothing, they would desire that life, which remains in exultation and knows no end. For this life is fleeting and so treacherous that it could not even keep faith with its lovers. From the beginning of the world, it

has deceived those who believed in it, it has misled all who expected it, it has mocked all who presumed upon it, and thus it has rendered no one certain, so that it may be proven to have lied to all. And if only it were subject solely to the fault of lying, and did not compel its lovers to run through all crimes. It gives gluttony to gluttons, it inflicts drunkenness on the drunken, it delivers the shipwreck of modesty to adulterers, it hands over the abominable depravity to the incestuous; it advises the thief to steal; the angry one to rage; the liar to deceive. It sows divorces among spouses, discord among friends, strife among the peaceful, injustice among the just, and scandals among brothers. It takes away justice from judges, chastity from the pure, skill from craftsmen; it removes discipline from morals. And to recall the greater crimes it instills in its lovers; if a brother ever kills a brother, if a son slays a father, if a friend is slain by a friend; by whose instigation have these crimes been committed, by whose gaze, by whose hope, by whose trust have these abominable deeds been done? Is it not seduced by the love of this present life that they commit these things, and while they love it more than is just, do they pursue men with unjust hatred? For what reason does the pirate slay the sailor, for what reason does the robber kill the traveler, does the rich oppress the poor, does the proud crush the humble, and does every harmful person burden the innocent? They do these evils because they desire to serve this life, and they believe themselves to endure in love of it for longer times. Therefore, no crime is committed for any other reason than that the most unfortunate carnal life may be served by the carnal.

11. It is indeed she who commands them crimes, orders misdeeds, persuades them to injustice; and after having been filled with all cruelty and all filth, she delivers those serving her to her daughter, that is, to perpetual death. For from her, and from her womb, eternal death was born, at the time when the first men served their gluttony, lust, and the delights of the eyes; and therefore, those who had been made for eternal life were thrown into this realm of death: from here

they were again cast down to hell, carrying nothing with them except sins. Therefore, this life is what deceives you, O most beloved friends, so that you unjustly recall your friends who are going to eternal life.

CHAPTER IV. The punishments of hell, the joys of heaven, impressed upon the souls of martyrs.

12. This instigates you, O most holy parents, to recall your departing children to the company of heaven, to the incorruptible honor, to the friendships of the eternal emperor, with the most foolish lamentations. This is what has made you, O most chaste wives of the Blessed, through the color of piety, betray the minds of the Martyrs, and bring death for liberation. For if they had consented to your recall, they could indeed have been with you for a short time; but afterward, they would be separated, and thus they would have been separated from you, so that you would never see them except amidst perpetual torments; where the devouring flame consumes the souls of the unbelievers, where the dragons eat the lips of the blasphemers, where serpents feed on the breasts of the unbelievers with their bites. There, howling and groaning resound, and confused cries, which the force of torments stirs up, and the burning of the fire extorts. This very tribulation, which will receive the unbelievers there, has no limit, no conclusion, but is not consumed even after the burning of the fierce flames, but is restored again to renewed fires for whoever has been burned.

13. Therefore, allow this punishment and those to escape, and think of rescuing yourselves. Meanwhile, allow them to reach the crown destined for them. Do not be afraid; for they will not be separated from you, but will go to prepare for you in heaven celestial mansions, in which you and your children may dwell in eternal joy. If your houses made of stones delight you, how much more should the beauty of those houses invite you, where the dining rooms shine with pure

gold, adorned with gems and pearls? The purple flower of roses never fades: there, the flowering groves bloom with perpetual greenness: there, the fresh meadows always flow with honeyed streams: there, the grass is fragrant with golden flowers, and the breathing fields are filled with most pleasant scents. The breezes there, having eternal life, waft a nectar-like fragrance to the nostrils. The light there shines without the sun's ray, serenity without clouds, and without the darkness of night, the eyes enjoy the day. There, the delights are not hindered by any occupation, nor is security disturbed by any anxiety; moos, howls, groans, lamentations, and grief are never heard or named there: the foul and deformed, the ugly, the black, the horrifying, or anything filthy have never been seen by the eyes of the inhabitants: but in the beauty of the pleasant groves, in the splendor of the cheerful air, and in the gracefulness and all elegance, the eyes are continuously delighted; and nothing at all that troubles the mind is given to the ears. For there, the organs of hymns sound continuously, sung in praise of the King by angels and archangels. Bitterness and the harshness of gall have no place there: thunder has never been heard there, nor have lightning and flashes ever appeared. Cinnamon bushes grow there, and balsam trees burst forth. The fragrance of the air spreads delight through all the members, and no food there produces filth. For just as the ears are nourished by good news, the nostrils by good scents, and the eyes by good sights, and this refreshment cannot break into digestion; so there, the refreshment, which the mouth receives, is honeyed in taste, pleasing to each one according to what he has delighted in. Finally, whatever the soul desires, all serve its desire, and the effects are most ready to serve all its pleasures.

14. For those who in this mortal life have fought against their desires and against pleasures, whoever has not spent them here, will obtain them intact from their Creator there. For He created man to live: and placed death next to the entrance of pleasure, so that those who wish to escape the fear of death may

seek eternal life; and when they have learned that there is another life beyond this one, they may inquire whether it can be cut off by old age or concluded by death: and when they have recognized it as immortal, they may inquire whether that eternity can again bestow honor upon the just or inflict punishment upon the unjust.

CHAPTER V. The Use of Wealth and Delights.

15. And when they have specifically proven that it is so, it remains to ask why wealth was created by the Creator if it is to be despised by His law, or why the variety of quadrupeds, birds, and creeping things was made by the Creator if each is to be renounced: why, moreover, is genuine delight deeply rooted in bodies as an incitement to lust by the Creator Himself, if its use not only makes the author guilty but also subjects him to eternal fires? Therefore, it is asked: Why were riches given by the Creator if they are to be despised? We respond: Those riches made by the Creator somehow speak to their lovers, saying: "Love us in such a way that we may never be separated from you." We cannot follow you dying; however, we can precede you living, but only if you command it. The greedy moneylender gives gold to a man to receive it back doubled, another sows different seeds in the earth, so that if it can happen, he may seek to receive back a hundredfold what he simply sows: and the debtor returns gold to the creditor doubled, and the earth yields back seeds a hundredfold. Alas! The debtor can pay back interest to the moneylender; and the earth can restore to the farmer seeds multiplied a hundredfold; can God, if He has received His riches from you, not return them to you multiplied?

16. You now inquire: Why did He give me riches if they are to be returned to Him? He entrusted them to you so that you may know how much rest, how much pleasure, how much luxury, and how many delights there can be in

them, so that by having love with your riches, you may yourself entrust them to be kept for our Lord Jesus Christ. If you do not wish to believe this, either the greed of gluttony will invade them, or the mother of lusts will snatch them from you, or without a doubt, as you know very well, death will unexpectedly seize you and will so wrest them from you that you will no longer foresee having or seeing them at all. If you were to pass through the midst of barbarian ranks and find a strong man who has always loved you, who even had given you a bag full of money, saying to you: "Give me the money I entrusted to you to keep, because these barbarians lie in wait to take it from you; when they have taken it, they will tear you apart with their swords," would you not fall at his feet and beg him to take it back, certain that he would return it to you in greater abundance than he had given, and would free you from your enemies? It remains now that you may have Christ as your guardian of your riches.

17. Let us come to delight. Whoever has ears to hear, let them hear them saying: If you are truly our lovers, commend us to Him who will restore us to you whole and unblemished in that region where we may remain with you continually: for in this life, if we wish to occupy your service, as if experienced here, we will utterly deny you our service there. Let us be allowed to serve those who are dying for the time being, for this is why the days of mortals are shortened, that we may serve the immortals continually. For it is written (Matthew 24:22): "For the elect's sake those days will be shortened, so that our service may not be long." Indeed, we serve unjustly in a hurried course: we serve the wicked, the sinful, and the vile, not willingly; but because of Him who has subjected us. Nevertheless, we will be freed from the bondage of corruption and will be called back to the freedom of the glory of the children of God. Therefore, every delight, reserved for the future life, is not lost; for the treasures that have been stored are not considered by Him who hid them on earth to be

of interest; but rather, He confidently possesses them all the more securely, the more secretly and safely He has placed them.

18. Therefore, let the abundance of all delights be reserved, so that they are not touched in this life, which is passing: for if they have been in use here, they will be lost in that life, which never passes. Suppose this life is stretched over a hundred years, will not the last day, when excluded, immediately seem as if it never was, and as if the trace of a guest who stayed with us for one day is left behind? However, that life remains continually and perseveres insistently, even growing younger and thriving as the years pass, and from there takes the beginning of renewal from where the end is received. O truly degenerate and devoid of all good, who is not captivated by the love of this so beautiful life! Who fears to give up this life, which is destined to perish, and to take that which knows not how to perish, in which delights and pleasures, and riches, and joys begin in such a way that they do not know an end; thus they begin, that they cannot entirely cease.

19. For whoever does not wish to be a lover of this most splendid life not only loses this one and does not reach that one, but also, as I have already said, is captured and held by perpetual death; in which there is a continuous flame, enduring tribulation, and eternal punishment; in which fierce angels dwell, whose arms are the heads of dragons, whose eyes shoot fiery arrows; whose teeth protrude like those of elephants, and sting to torment like the tails of scorpions, whose voices sound like the roar of lions, whose appearance instills both tremor and pain and death. And would that death intervene in these dire straits! But what is more bitter, it is lived so that it is governed by torments, it is renewed so that the limbs are continually touched by the gnawing bites of serpents, repeated again and again.

CHAPTER VI. The Happiness and Glory of Martyrs.

20. This is the whole reason for the contest, which teaches that the penalties of martyrdom should be endured more tolerably. Therefore, do not, O friends, do not, O parents, do not, O spouses of the venerable saints, recall those whom you love from life to death, lead them from joy to mourning, drag them from light to darkness, and summon them from eternal rest to everlasting punishments. This is like casting a hook to fish with the devil, inviting to a small sweetness, in which the torment of the innermost being lies hidden, and the death of the inner self is extorted by torment. Is it not to prefer fleeting joys to the compensation of eternal delights; and to have them laugh a little, to bind them to eternal tears? This we condemn in gladiators, who willingly offer themselves, considering the delights of one year, and do not consider what fruits arise from those delights. And they are tormented by the blows of swords, or by the alternating slaughter of their inner being, exposing their torn bellies before the people, so that the fatness which thoughtless feeding had provided, may be offered to the devil to be devoured. By this counsel of the enemy, by which they do these things, the martyrs of God going to eternal life are recalled, who are implored to endure perpetual torments in exchange for a life of a few days, and not to fear the death that is especially to be dreaded.

21. To this place you may perhaps add: Why does a Christian not fear torture, and is not terrified by the present punishment of the torturer? Therefore, he is not broken by fear, therefore he is not led by pain, because he knows that he buys the joy of perpetual health with the price of a single pain; and through momentary tribulation, he reaches everlasting happiness and eternal joy. But if this pain is to be feared, the executioner is to be feared, and also the new and exquisite cruelty of the torturer; which is more to be feared, which is horrendous, which is more to be fled from, and to be avoided, that which today

seethes, and tomorrow vanishes? Today blazes, and tomorrow cools? That which is introduced for an hour, and excluded for an hour? Or that which is concluded by no end, extinguished by no time, consumed by no old age at all? For this pain is either light, and can be tolerably endured; or it is grave, and offers a glorious contest as a swift end; but that pain of punishments and torments of fire, which is given to the lovers of this life, since it is more intense than all kinds of torments, never ceases to attack, and grows fiercer than it began, and there is no limit to its savagery, no end at all occurs, but having all kinds of punishments with it, it is renewed again and again to rage, increased to torture, inflamed to burn more fiercely.

22. Therefore, from this destruction, let us urge those we love to escape; and let us prepare ourselves to escape bravely: nor let us fear to bear pain in the body for one hour, who wish to rejoice eternally with Christ, let us allow our soul to depart from this body with the palm of martyrdom, so that we may escape eternal punishments and reach the heavenly possessions full of delights. Let us turn our tears into joy: for we ought not to mourn as if we were about to die, those whom we believe will reign with Christ. Let us rejoice with the victors of the enemies, their necks trampled upon: let us rejoice in the garments of martyrdom, and let us glory in having become consuls of heaven. Behold the day in which the tyrant thought he could conquer himself, who while capturing, was captured; while holding, was bound; while torturing, was tortured: while he insults, he is mocked; while he slaughters, he is slain. Now therefore, in the love of martyrdom, let us also raise our affections; so that we may seize him who wished to take victory from our captivity, and as if awakened from a heavy sleep, let us open the eyes of our souls, so that seeing the traps which the enemy had prepared for our destruction, we, with God's help, may escape, and the devil himself, with his satellites, may fall into the very

pit he had prepared, let us say with the prophet: They have dug a pit before my face, and they have fallen into it themselves (Ps. 56:7).

CHAPTER VII. By the prayer and miracles of Sebastian, Zoe and Nicostratus are converted.

23. Therefore, when the most blessed Sebastian, clothed in a cloak, girded with a belt, was speaking these things from his own mouth, he was suddenly illuminated by an excessive brightness coming from heaven for almost one hour, and under that brightness, he was clothed by seven most radiant angels in a most brilliant robe, and a young man appeared beside him giving him peace, and saying: You will always be with me.

24. However, these things were happening inside the house of the Primicerius, named Nicostratus, where Marcellianus and Marcus were being kept. This Nicostratus had a wife named Zoe: she had become mute six years ago due to excessive illness, yet she had not lost the ability to hear and understand; rather, she was now able to comprehend better than she had before. Therefore, when she understood everything that Blessed Sebastian had said and saw such light around him; and when all were held in awe by the wonder of the miracle, she gestured with her hand to everyone, as if to reproach those who did not believe such evident assertion, and, falling to her knees, began to beseech him with gestures of her hands. But Saint Sebastian, seeing that she could not express the secrets of her heart with her tongue, inquired about the cause of her silence and learned that the abundance of speech had been taken from her by the excessive force of her illness. Then Blessed Sebastian said: If I am a true servant of Christ, and if all that this woman has heard and believed from my mouth is true, may my Lord Jesus Christ command that her tongue return to her, and may He open the mouth of her who opened the mouth of His prophet Zachariah; and

he made the sign of the cross on her mouth. At this word of Saint Sebastian, the woman cried out with a loud voice, saying: Blessed are you, and blessed is the word of your mouth: and blessed are those who believe in Christ, the Son of the living God, through you. For I have seen with my own eyes an angel coming to you from heaven, holding a book before your eyes, from the reading of which the entire prayer of your speech flowed. Blessed are those who believe in all that you have spoken, and cursed are those who have doubted even in one word of all that they have heard: for just as the dawn, coming, excludes all the darkness of the night and restores the light that the blind night denied to all eyes; so the light of your words has wiped away all gloom and all blindness of ignorance, and has restored a clear day to the eyes of those who rightly believe, while it has not only excluded the darkness of my unbelief but also opened the door of my speech, which had been closed for six years.

25. However, seeing that such virtue of Christ was celebrated in his wife, Nicostratus, her husband, began to fall at her feet and to seek forgiveness for having had the Saints of God in chains by imperial and prefectural order: and taking the iron bonds from their hands, embracing their knees, he began to plead that they would deign to depart, saying: O how blessed would I be if I could be bound for your salvation! Perhaps by the shedding of my blood I would be washed away, so that I might escape that death of eternal punishments and reach that life which God has deemed worthy to manifest to us through the mouth of my lord Sebastian.

CHAPTER VIII. The steadfastness of Marcellianus and Marcus, a prayer to the neophytes.

26. And when he asked Marcellianus and Marcus to depart, they said to him: If you have received the glory of faith, which you never had; how can we, who

have always had such faith since childhood, abandon it, and give you the cup of our passion, which we can offer you, not donate? For Christ is rich in all, and the abundance of His bounty offers better things to all who come than what is asked. For if, when you were unbelievers, the light of truth was granted to you to recognize; how much more will all that you now ask be granted to you who believe? For divine mercy is always ready to freely provide for all of you: and the more one receives the gift of His grace, the more elevated his mind has accepted the standard of higher faith. Therefore, your faith took its beginning from teaching, and all that ancient learning scarcely imparts, you have grasped in the span of one hour. No memory of parents hinders you from believing. No nurturing affection recalls tender age in your sons and daughters. Suddenly you disdain what you have always loved and seek what you have never known. Having entered unknown paths, you have suddenly come to Christ, and with your mind you have already entered heaven, because you have sought no solace on earth. O incomparable proclamation of deeds! O how imitable an example of virtue! You have not yet been led to Christ by the wave of sacred baptism, you have not yet taken at least the signs of military initiation; and already you take up arms for the true King and desiring to free yourselves from the bonds of iron, you wish to be fearless in order to be killed for killing.

27. When all heard these things, they showed repentance for their past persuasion with tears, Marcus said: Learn, dearest parents, and may your conjugal affection learn, O spouses, to oppose the fight of the devil, and to place the shield of virtues against all the arrows of carnal desire, and not to yield to the ranks of the tyrannical army, to fight more fiercely, to hold your ground, and to reach the King bravely. Let the satellites of demons rise as much as they want, and rage, and tear our bodies with whatever punishments they wish; they can kill the body, but they cannot conquer the soul that fights for the truth of faith. Wounds received for the emperor make soldiers more glorious: for in this

the devil now rages with the fury of his tyranny, in which he foresees that he can be tormented by the trophy of your perseverance: and therefore, he inflicts torments, lest his hope perish: he threatens death to frighten; he promises life to snatch away; he promises security to take away. This entire cunning of war, this plan of deceit, is to seize the body from torments and to subjugate the soul to vices. Let us, on the contrary, strive not to yield to the enemy, to disdain the body, to assist the soul. For why should the most valiant leaders turn their backs on the most miserable soldiers, and fail in that battle in which they can be victors? Or for what reason should they fear to die, who knows that this is human nature, not punishment? Why, I say, should they fear to die, who believe that this life is false, and that true life cannot be found unless one has rejected this falsehood from his soul, and the fleeting one, which offers nothing to its lovers except sins, urges crimes; and demands nothing else from its lovers than to not think at all about eternal life, and to despair of the future kingdom of God?

28. Now let us see what cases she is subject to, and what dangers the maidservant endures, so that when we have proven her unable to govern herself, we may seek another whom we ought justly to serve, removing our servitude from her dominion. For how many lovers has her sudden and heavy downfall crushed, how many has the crash of heaven struck, how many has lightning ignited, how many have been lost to shipwrecks, how many has chaos covered, how many has Charybdis swallowed, how many has the sword slaughtered! And those wretched ones, losing life with pain, cannot find her at all! For indeed, torture does not lead to that life, but cause does. Ultimately, by the same kind of punishment, eternal salvation is granted to the innocent, and punishment is inflicted on the guilty.

CHAPTER IX. The others converted by Sebastian along with the captives. 29. Therefore, as Marcus was recounting these things and similar matters, all those present began to give thanks to God, and all, weeping, expressed their sorrow for having preferred the love of the flesh over the love of God; and because they had dared to withdraw their souls from the struggle of martyrdom. And when all who had come to deceive the saints unanimously believed in Christ, Nicostratus, with his wife, urged himself, saying: I will neither eat food nor drink, unless the mystery of the Christian religion is revealed to me. To him, Saint Sebastian said: Change your dignity, and begin to be more of a Christian than a prefect. Therefore, heed my counsel, and gather together all those whom the prison confines, whom the chains hold, whom the labor camps torment, into one. When you have done this, I will summon the bishop of the most sacred law, so that you may receive the sacrament of the mystery with all who wish to believe. For if the devil has attempted and continues to attempt to take away the saints from Christ, how much more should we, by the argument of piety, care for those whom the devil has unjustly gained and restore them to their Creator? And Nicostratus replied to this, saying: How can the holy be entrusted to the wicked and the criminal? Saint Sebastian said: Our Savior has deemed it worthy to present His presence to us for sinners and shows the mystery through which all sins and crimes are taken away from man, and all the virtues of the Lord are conferred. Therefore, at the beginning of your conversion, if you offer this gift to Christ, the reward of His remuneration will be present upon you, the crown of martyrdom, having with it the unfading flowers of all virtues, which will be beneficial for the joys of eternal life. Hearing this, Nicostratus, the prefect, went to Claudius the Commentarian and ordered all the people to be brought to his house, saying: Since in the next session all are to be discussed, I want them to be present with those Christians who are with me, so that no person may be absent from any discussion of the prefect.

30. Therefore, when all were brought to the house of the prefect, bound by the chains, the man of God, Sebastian, spoke to them in this way: If the diabolical crimes yield to divine virtues, your guilt is excluded from death and is recalled from fleeting joys. For the unjust enemy had acted through his satellites, seeking to overthrow the souls of Christ's soldiers, raised to the peak of virtue, and attempting to drown them in the mire of hell. For this reason, the spirit of the enemies was ignited, provoked by the struggle, so that you, whom the enemy had already gained, might be taken from his captivity and returned to your Creator. For the devil is neither your lord, nor creator, nor father: but God, and Father, and Lord, and Creator is proven. And if, leaving Him, you have gone to him who has been such an enemy to you that he has led you to the punishments of eternal death, and made you come to this lethal end; how much more must you return to Him who delivered His only Son to passion and death, so that He might free us from eternal sufferings and from perpetual death? As Saint Sebastian was recounting these things and similar matters, all fell prostrate with tears, and bending their knees, began to give a groan of the heart, and cried out with voices of repentance that they had sinned and acted wickedly. Therefore, they poured forth bitter tears, and with unanimous voices, they resounded that they wished to believe in Christ. Then Blessed Sebastian commanded that all be freed from the bonds of the chains.

CHAPTER X. All prepared for baptism by Polycarp.

31. After these things, Saint Sebastian went to the presbyter Polycarp, where there was a hidden cause of persecution, and he narrated to him all that had happened. Upon hearing these things, Saint Polycarp gave thanks to God, and together with him went to the house of Nicostratus the primicerius, and seeing the crowds of believers, greeting them with all joy he said: Blessed are all of you who have heard the voice of our Lord Jesus Christ saying: Come to me all you

who labor and are heavy laden, and I will give you rest. Take my yoke upon you, and learn from me, for I am gentle and lowly in heart; and you will find rest for your souls. For my yoke is easy, and my burden is light (Matt. 9:28). Therefore, you, our brothers, whom the wave of baptism has not yet washed, and who have been made beloved sons of Almighty God through consecration, because you have attempted to turn back the most blessed soldiers of Christ from the holy purpose, you needed repentance, so that through it you might come to indulgence. But now, since you have attained such glory, that you even desired to run willingly and to embrace the passion from which you wished to turn others back with sorrow, know that you have reached indulgence and are about to attain the palm. This is the ancient craft of Christ. For Him whom He deemed worthy of His choice and wished to give as a teacher to the nations, who not only turned the minds of the faithful from the purpose of piety, but also buried those unwilling to depart from Christ in stones; this same Lord has bestowed upon us the apostle, and has given us Paul from Saul, making him an apostle from an apostate, and has given the Church from a persecutor a teacher. He became a lover of passion who had been the author of persecution: and he who had previously rejoiced in the afflictions of others, later rejoiced in his own persecutions. Therefore, He who then exercised this power in His apostle, He also now from the infernal abyss, and from the jaws of the dragons has rescued the captivity of your souls and has now opened to you the gates of eternal life as you return from darkness to light. Therefore, since all demons, who are the children of darkness, are saddened, hence all holy angels, who are the children of light, rejoice; let each of you come forward and give his name, so that today, throughout the day until evening, the fasting may find an opportune time for the festive sacrament of baptism. For it is just that as light departs from the mortal world, it approaches our immortal minds, so that we who are rolled in the mud of darkness in this world, washed and cleansed by the water of sanctification, and clothed in sincerity may cheerfully proceed to Christ. With these and similar words, all rejoiced at the exhortation of Saint Polycarp, and each one hurried to offer his name before he was asked.

CHAPTER XI. The baptized catechumens, together with Claudius and his sons.

32. While these things were happening, Claudius the commentariensis came to the house of the primicerius Nicostratus, where these things were being done; and he said to Nicostratus: The prefecture has been greatly disturbed because you have ordered the persons of the accused to be handed over to your house's custody. For this reason, the prefect has commanded you to be presented before him. See that you must give a response as if you were being interrogated. Therefore, when Nicostratus entered before the prefect and was asked why he wished the persons whom the prison's confines were holding to be placed under his custody, he replied: By your command, I have received Christian persons to be kept within my house, whom I made to associate with the accused to instill fear of punishment, so that they might consent, if not by their own accord, at least by the experience of others, and fear that a similar punishment might befall them. The prefect, hearing this gladly, dismissed him, saying: I will ensure that you are rewarded greatly by their parents, since through you their sons have been restored unharmed.

33. Therefore, returning to his house, Nicostratus the primicerius began to recount everything to Claudius the commentariensis, and how Saint Sebastian, being a friend of the emperors, is most Christian, and perfected in divine knowledge, and how he had recalled the souls of Christians by his exhortation, and that he had sufficiently taught that this life is fleeting and imaginary, and thus while being held, it is taken away. He also narrated how suddenly light

from heaven illuminated him, and how his wife, who had been mute for six years, was made to speak.

34. When Nicostratus had narrated these things to Claudius, Claudius fell at the feet of Nicostratus, saying: I have two sons from my deceased wife, one of whom is afflicted by dropsy, the other is oppressed by various wounds; I ask that you command them to be visited. For I do not doubt that He who was able to make your wife speak after six years will, if He wills, restore health to my sons. Saying this, he rushed to his house and had his two sons brought before him, and bringing them into the house where the holy ones of God were, he threw them before their feet, saying: No signs of doubt whatever remain in my heart: but believing with all my heart that Christ, whom you worship, is the true God, I have brought you my two increments, believing that they might be freed from the danger of death through you. All the holy ones of God said to him together: All those who are held here today by some illness will be healed as soon as they become Christians.

35. And as Claudius cried out that he believed and desired to become a Christian, Saint Polycarp commanded that each should give his name. Therefore, the first of all gave his name as Tranquillinus, father of Marcellian and Marcus. After him, six of their friends, that is, Ariston, Crescentianus, Eutychianus, Urbanus, Vitalis, and Justus; after these, Nicostratus the primicerius, and his brother Castorius, and Claudius the commentariensis. After these, the sons of Claudius, Felicissimus and Felix. After these, Marcia, mother of Marcellian and Marcus, with their wives and children: and also Symphorosa, the wife of Claudius, and Zoe, the wife of Nicostratus. After these, the whole household that was in the house of Nicostratus, thirty-three souls of mixed sex and age, then all who had been bound, and brought from the filth of the prison, sixteen souls.

36. Therefore, all those sixty-eight were baptized by St. Polycarp the presbyter and received by St. Sebastian; among the women, Beatrix and Lucina became mothers. Thus, first the sons of Claudius, one suffering from dropsy and the other full of wounds, were soon immersed in the name of the Holy Trinity; so they were raised up healthy from the fountain that not even a sign of any past illness remained in them. After these infants, Tranquillinus, the father of St. Marcellian and Mark, who was so afflicted by gout and sciatica that, as previously mentioned, he could scarcely be carried in the arms. As they were removing his garments, and he was saying that he was tormented by intolerable pain, Polycarp the presbyter asked him, saying: Tranquillinus, if you believe with all your heart that the only begotten Son of God, our Lord Jesus Christ, can grant you salvation and forgive all your sins, proclaim it with your own mouth. Tranquillinus replied: I desire and believe that forgiveness alone for my sins is granted to me. Moreover, even if after this sanctification of baptism I should suffer in pain, I will not be able to doubt further in the faith of Christ: for I have proven and, believing with all my heart, I have consented in my mind that the Son of God is our Lord Jesus Christ, who can grant salvation to both souls and bodies, and recall from eternal death to everlasting life. When he had said this with a loud voice, all the saints shed tears of joy, and they prayed to the Lord that the fruits of his faith might be shown. Therefore, St. Polycarp the confessor and presbyter, as soon as he anointed him with the chrism, asked him again if he believed in the Father and the Son and the Holy Spirit; as soon as he replied, I believe, his hands, which were knotted, were loosened, and his knees and the soles of his feet were restored to health, so that as if a little boy, renewing his feet, he descended into the fountain, crying out and saying: You are the one true God, whom this wretched world does not know.

37. Thus, in their proper order, all were baptized as was fitting, and for the ten days that remained of the delay they had earned, they spent day and night in

hymns and songs in praise of God, and like faithful soldiers prepared their souls to fight for the name of Christ in martyrdom, so that in both women and infants the love of martyrdom burned, and they prepared one another for the confession of the holy name against the diabolical ranks.

CHAPTER XII. The errors of the Gentiles were refuted before Chromatius, the prefect of the city, by Tranquillinus.

38. Therefore, when the days of the granted delay were fulfilled, Agrestius Chromatius, the prefect of the city of Rome, ordered Tranquillinus, the father of Marcellian and Mark, to come to him. When he inquired about the judgment of his sons, Tranquillinus replied: No speech of mine is sufficient to express gratitude for your benefits. For unless the reins of your governance had held the running sentences, I would have lost my sons, and they would not have had me as their father. All those whose paternal affection holds rejoice with me, and the sting of charity pricks; I believe also that your highness rejoices with me, when life is granted to those about to die, and joy is restored to the anxious, and security is given back to the troubled.

39. Then the prefect, thinking that his sons wished to bow their necks to idols, said: Therefore, on the appointed day, let your sons offer incense to the gods: through which both you and your sons may continue safe, and your sons may be forgiven. Hearing this, Tranquillinus said: Most illustrious of men, if you wish to weigh with an equal balance your judgment against me and my sons, you will be able to recognize that this Christian name is of great virtue. The prefect said: You are insane, Tranquillinus. Tranquillinus replied: I have suffered insanity, both of soul and body; but as soon as I believed in Christ, I received health for my soul and body.

40. The prefect said: I see that I have granted these terms to your wicked sons, so that not only would you not remove them from error, but they would ensnare you with their errors. Tranquillinus said: By your glory, examine the very name of error, and see what works are now called by the name of error. The prefect said: You say what works and take the name of error. Tranquillinus said: The first error is to abandon the way of life and willingly walk the way of death. The prefect said: And what is the way of death? Tranquillinus said: Do you not see that it is the way of death to impose the name of divinity upon dead men and to worship their images through wood and stone?

41. The prefect said: Therefore, are there not gods whom we worship? Tranquillinus said: They are not gods to such an extent that it is read in public records, and how poorly they were born, and what wicked and cruel parents they had; and how unjustly and deceitfully and fraudulently they lived; and how miserably they died. Was there not a God in heaven before Saturn ruled the Cretans and ate the flesh of his sons, or did the island of Crete have a king and the heavens not have a God? He greatly errs who thinks Jupiter, his son, rules with thunderbolts, a little man in whom malice and lust reigned. Who did not pursue him, who spared not his father? Or what filth did he not commit, who took his own sister as his wife? In the forum, in the streets, in the houses, and in every place, we read daily that the most sordid Juno boasts of being both sister and wife: and the honor of the abducted Ganymede, the most shameful and incestuous, is not denied by those from whom Jupiter is worshiped. Therefore, you do not err, most sublime man, who worship such beings, as the Roman laws command to be condemned according to the quality of their deeds, and leaving aside the Almighty God who reigns in heaven, you say to a stone, You are my God: and to wood, Help me?

42. The prefect said: Since you began to blaspheme the gods and to withdraw from their worship, from that time the Roman world is oppressed by various calamities. Tranquillinus replied: It is not true. For if you review the decades compiled in the style of Livy, you will find there offerings of incense to Jupiter, and in one day twenty-three thousand young men of the Roman army fell. But also do not forget that the Senones Gauls occupied the Capitol and subjected the entire Roman force to their mockery. The Roman world has suffered various famines, and unspeakable plagues, various captivities, various outpourings of blood, before men worshiped one God. Now indeed, since the invisible and true God began to be worshiped by believers, the Roman empire rejoices in increased peace. But what is worse, the God who provides this is not recognized; rather, what is provided by the Creator is attributed to His creatures.

43. The prefect said: If He is to be worshiped who provides something for human benefits, then only the sun will be considered a god, who invigorates the earth's depths with its sight, so that the seeds taken up may give birth, and restores the grains of the genuine offspring in the stalk, and grants both light and restoration equally to all the utilities of our salvation. Tranquillinus replied: And in this, there is infinite error. For if today someone through his servant grants what is requested to his clients, it is infinite foolishness if the neglected one who provided it is honored, the servant through whom it was provided. And to present some comparison for this saying; when Roman ships bring food, are thanks given to the ships rather than to the kings? Therefore, if not to the navigators, but to the rulers, do men attribute what is announced, how much more should thanks be given solely to God, whose nod serves all these elements for our uses, and the sun itself is daily both enclosed at the end of the day and opened again at the renewal of the day?

THE ACTS OF ST. SEBASTIAN

CHAPTER XIII. The Incarnation of the Word Explained to the Gentile. 44. The prefect said: If therefore there is one and invisible whom you worship, you do not worship Christ, whom the Jews crucified? Tranquillinus said: You would inquire rightly if you intended to believe. For the unbelievers, everything they do not want seems vain. For once the will of mortals declines headlong, it desires to be blamed for everything it blames; and it wants everything it praises to be praised by all. But the wise, according to their merit, either strive to impose blame or praise on anything. The prefect said: I ask you about your Christ. If indeed what is worshiped by you is not seen by these eyes, do you not worship Christ who was seen, and heard, and questioned, and all that pertains to human fragility is read in His completed passion? Tranquillinus said: Listen to the analogy and understand the truth: For example, if today you see your ring with a precious gem rolling in a sewer, or wallowing in dung, and you send your servants to retrieve it; but they are unable to free it, and while trying to rescue it, they have soiled themselves; then you yourself, laying aside these silken garments you are wearing, put on a servant's tunic and descending into the sewer, put your hands in the filth, and at the same time you represent the golden ring with your hands and the gem, you invite all your friends to a feast in joy and rejoice over the ring and gem, that they have been freed from excessive filth. The prefect said: To what likeness have you brought this proposition? Tranquillinus replied: To show you that we worship one invisible God. The prefect said: And what is gold? Or what is the gem that was rolling in the dung? Tranquillinus replied: Gold is the human body, and the gem is the soul, which is enclosed in that body. But the body and soul make one man, just as gold and gems are proven to make one ring. But however precious the ring may be to you, a man is far more precious, a hundredfold, and dear to Christ. You sent your servants to rescue the ring from the filth, and they could not possibly rescue it. God sent His prophets from heaven speaking to them, to rescue the human race from the filth of this world: and they could not at all do this by any means. You laid aside golden garments, and clothed in a servant's garment descended into the sewer, and put your hands in the filth to free the ring from the filth: He stripped Himself of the splendor of His divine majesty, yet did not leave the heavenly realm; and clothed Himself with the garment of our servant body, and here in the sewer of this world descending from heaven, put His hands in the filth of our passions; and receiving the passion that was owed to us by our merits, He restored us to the glory of His fingers. For those who were rolling in the filth of the world through unbelief, washed clean from the filth by faith, are restored by divine hands, just like your ring. Did your servants, who denied their master while they looked at Him in the form of a servant, not have the power to kill Him as rebels? So too, those who deny Christ their Lord because He emptied Himself of majesty and took the form of a servant, will by no means be able to escape the pains of eternal fire. Therefore, finally, for us who believe in Him, the wave of the eternal fountain comes to our aid, so that the eternal fire may be vanquished by the eternal fountain, and unbelief may be overcome by faithfulness.

45. The prefect said: As I see it, you are not asking to be released from this intention for the sake of your sons, but to bring these silly tales to our tribunals. Tranquillinus said: The disciples of Christ do not meditate on what they should say in the presence of judges. For He had foretold saying: When they deliver you up to the authorities of this world for my name's sake, do not think about how or what you should speak, for it will be given to you in that hour what you should say. For it is not you who speak, but the Spirit of God who speaks in you (Matt. 10:19). Therefore, it is not by meditating that I found my Creator, but by believing; and I who was afflicted by gout and arthritis, as soon as I believed in Christ, received health in all my limbs as if I were a little child. It is therefore established in my mind that He who deigned to renew me is the same who created me, and just as He gave restoration to my body, so He has

also promised to give it to my soul after this life, provided that I am not broken by the terror of men, nor doubting or timid; but enduring in the confession of His name, I will keep the complete faith that God made me find.

46. The prefect said: You do not know, Tranquillinus, how great is the fury of the invincible princes against Christians, and therefore you pursue what seems secure to you without fear. Tranquillinus said: It is a foolish fear, by which human indignation is feared more than divine. If we come into the midst of barking dogs, and they begin to attack us with their bites in vain fury, can they take away from our minds what we are rational beings, while they are dogs, irrational and insane? Thus, those who are angry with us who believe rightly can indeed rage and inflict unjust punishments; however, they can never take from our hearts what we believe, that the Lord Jesus Christ is our Creator, and we rejoice that He is our Redeemer and Restorer. Then the prefect ordered him to be taken from the records, saying: I will hear you at the next session.

CHAPTER XIV. Chromatius, the prefect of the city, is catechized.

47. After this, he sent for him to be brought to him secretly at night, and offering him an immense weight of gold, he said: Show me the remedy by which you recovered your health. To which Tranquillinus said: Know that a great wrath and fury of God will be endured by those who think His grace can be sold or bought. Therefore, if you wish to be freed from gout, believe in Christ the Son of God, and you will be freed, and just as you see me today, so you will be safe. Indeed, I could hardly be carried, and for eleven years I was bound by the knots of pain throughout all the joints of my body; hardly was bread handed to my mouth by the hands of others: as soon as I believed that Christ is the true God, I received the joys of my salvation, and I am unharmed because I recognized the true God as my Savior.

48. Then the prefect released him, saying: Bring to me the one who made you a Christian, so that if he promises me healing, I too may become a Christian. Immediately, Tranquillinus went to St. Polycarp the priest and told him all that had happened or been said; and leading him secretly into the house, he presented him to the sight of the prefect. To whom the prefect said: Although there is a serious animosity of the princes against Christians, nevertheless, in hope of recovering health, I will offer you whatever it is up to half of my estate, if my body's members are released from this knot of condylomata. Then St. Polycarp, smiling, said: The Lord Jesus Christ is able to open the doors of your ignorance and show you that He is the restorer of your body. For money, whether brought by those who offer it or received by those who accept it, does not only provide no medicine for the suffering, but they also take upon themselves an incurable disease. The prefect said to him: Tell me then what I should do to achieve what I hope for. Polycarp said to him: If you believe with all your heart, as Tranquillinus believed, you will be saved. The prefect said to him: In what order should I believe? Then St. Polycarp catechized him and instructed him to fast for three days. And calling St. Sebastian to him, he fasted with him for three days and three nights; and they prayed together with tears, that the Lord would reveal the faith of His name to the one wishing to believe for his salvation.

CHAPTER XV. The idols of Chromatius are broken.

49. Therefore, when the third day, which had been appointed, arrived, they came together hastening to the house of the prefect. And entering, they said: Peace to your faith. But he greeted them very politely; and he encouraged them to sit beside him, and said: From the mouth of Tranquillinus, the reason is declared by the assertion of my eyes. For I see this very healthy man who I had seen afflicted by gout and arthritis. Inquiring from him what kind of medicine

he had been saved by, I received such a response from him: While I placed my faith in idols, I was weak and afflicted by excessive infirmity; but when I learned to know the one God in heaven through the demonstration of Christians, I renounced all that I had worshiped without cause, and I entrusted the faith of my soul to Christ. But as soon as I confessed that the one true God reigns in heaven, immediately all the health that I had lost for eleven years returned to me, and all infirmity was immediately separated from me. I have heard this with my ears, I have proven it with my eyes, I have believed it with my heart; it remains that you do for Tranquillinus and me what you have done, so that I may receive health for my body.

50. The priest Polycarp said: If the pains of the soul of man do not endure, what will those pains do, of which there is never any end, and no succession is given at all? For these pains bear the image of those pains, and as much as there is a difference between a living fire and its picture, so much is the difference between the pains that the body suffers now, and those that the soul will suffer, if it has fulfilled the duty of this present life ignorant of its Creator. Come therefore with us first about those pains, and be concerned about that punishment, which has a fire always burning, and a worm always eating.

51. Then Chromatius, the prefect of the city of Rome, with his only son Tiburtius, gave his name, saying: It is fitting for you to be certain of my faith, in which I also desire that my son become a Christian with me. St. Sebastian said: See that you do not hope to become a Christian merely by the recovery of your body, but rather make your mind pure with the hope of eternal life to see the reason of truth. For unless you recognize who your Creator is, you will not be able to find the salvation you seek. Chromatius said: Do we not see that both rustic and very simple men are Christians, so that among a thousand men you can scarcely find one who can even acquire the discipline of speech? Were all

these able to reach that inquiry when they became Christians? St. Sebastian said: Your response confirms our assertion. For from the beginning of the world, God had dealings with farmers and shepherds of sheep, and coming near the end of the world, He did not choose grammarians and orators, but fishermen and simple men, and He entrusted His knowledge to them.

52. Chromatius said: Why then do you say that I must first recognize who my creator is, whom unless I recognize I cannot find salvation? St. Sebastian said: Because you have worshiped many gods and many goddesses. Therefore, unless you cast these out from your heart, and break their images, and recognize the one true God, you will not be able to find life and salvation. Chromatius said: Therefore, indicate to me who is the one true God. St. Sebastian responded: If you send your servant to draw water, when he comes to the fountain, he first looks to see if any filth is lurking inside the jar, and he does not dare to put water into the vessel unless he sees it cleansed from dirt; how can we deliver to you the fountain of truth, unless you first make yourself alien to all the filth and squalor of idols? Chromatius said: And in what order can I become alien from these? St. Sebastian said: Grant us the power to break all the idols that we find in your house, to burn the wooden ones, to melt the golden, silver, or brass ones, and to distribute their value to the needy. Chromatius said: And when you have done this, what benefit will come to me? St. Sebastian said: You will immediately achieve the health of all your nerves, which are constrained by their knots; and as if you had never been in pain, you will begin to run with your feet, and recognize that you have loved the gods who are enemies of your salvation; but this one, who restores and saves you as soon as you find His knowledge and worship, is your true parent.

53. Chromatius said: Do not lay this injury upon yourselves: but I will command my servants; and they will break everything. St. Sebastian said: If the

doubtful, timid, and unfaithful break them, the devil will find an occasion to harm them through any negligence of theirs, and as soon as they are harmed, the unfaithful will say that they were harmed because they broke the idols. For unless one has armor, he is not snatched away from the blows of arrows. For a skilled hand uses a helmet and shield and spear in battle, so that from the protection of arms and the impetus of striking, it may take on courage and not turn its back. Likewise, the soldiers of God, who are fortified with the shield of faith and protected by the armor of Christ, having the helmet of faith and salvation, it is safe for them to enter the contest. For they fight fiercely and strongly win, because they battle against an invisible enemy day and night without tiring; and they are covered in all their members, armed more by faith than by iron. Chromatius said: May the will of God and yours be done. Then St. Polycarp the priest, and Blessed Sebastian, girding themselves, prayed; and after the prayer, breaking more than two hundred signs of idols, they began to give thanks to their God.

CHAPTER XVI. Chromatius is healed after breaking the instruments of judicial astrology.

54. After these things, they approached Chromatius, saying to him: You should have received healing when the idols were broken, unless perhaps some signs of unfaithfulness remain in your mind. For we hold it certain among us that either there is something that has not yet been broken; or if everything is broken, what you harbor in your mind is more evident to us. Then he said: I have, he said, a glass chamber, in which all the discipline of the stars and mechanical mathematics is artfully constructed, in the making of which my father Tarquin is said to have spent more than two hundred pounds of gold. To which St. Sebastian said: If you wish to keep this intact, you are breaking yourself. Chromatius said: For what? Is mathematics or an ephemeris honored by some

use of sacrifices, when only the courses of months and years are distinguished by a certain number through the spaces of hours? And is the fullness or diminution of the lunar sphere foreseen by the motion of fingers, the mastery of reason, and the computation of calculation? St. Polycarp the priest said: There are the signs of Leo and Capricorn and Sagittarius, and Scorpio, and Taurus there, there in Aries the moon, in Cancer the hour; in Jupiter the star, in Mercury the tropic, in Venus Mars, and in all these monstrous demons, the art is known to be hostile to God. Christians refuse these things so much that they not only do not have them, do not honor them, do not believe in them, do not hold them; but they do not even have the spirit to occupy their hearts with such trifles? For all these are false and ministers of deception: the resemblance in them is of truth, not the truth itself.

55. Chromatius said to him: What? that they sometimes predict the future? St. Sebastian said: We have known that all these are the most vain and false, revealed by Christ; which we will now open to you more clearly. Command today a teacher of mathematics to come to you, to whom you should say that at that time you have suffered from harsh cases, and inquire through which stars this evil has happened to you; his answers will undoubtedly be such that your time has been taken up by malicious Mars, or Saturn has been apocatastically in effect, or your year has been taken from the diameter, or climacteric events have been born in your center, or there has been a conjunction with evil, or it has been invisible, or in a scheme, or the course in the stars has remained immobile around you. When he has said these things and similar ones, he tries to assign you something plausible in reason and prove it. Come now, ask another mathematician, to whom you should say that the very hours and the very time have flourished in good cases for you, immediately you will see him bring you infinite reasonable schemes, by which he will prove that good things ought to have happened to you in those times. For he holds a circle collected from every

side, in which he receives various and diverse causes, and from which he seizes the opportunity to say what he wants.

56. For while they cannot foresee the future deeply, they speak of climacterics, that is, uncertain escapes of nature. For those born at different times perished in one shipwreck, and one hour of day or night having arisen, one is cast into begging, another ascends to the kingdom: and in one battle an innumerable multitude is laid low, and in one day, indeed in one moment, in one house, two women, one becoming the most chaste, the other becoming impudent: if the stars of either have conferred merit, neither is the prostitute to be blamed, nor is the chaste one to be praised. Certainly, the bearers of laws and the princes punish their sacred transgressions, and therefore there is a forum, therefore a judge, therefore laws, so that the just may be rightly praised, and the unjust may be punished justly. And I do not want you to consider this as idle, that you see yourself not yet saved. For if you were to completely reject the ceremonies of the enemies of the human race, you would have learned in yourself what is true.

57. Hearing these things, Chromatius said: That true God is He who is proven to have such worshipers. For all your discourse flows so much with reason; that it inclines even the minds of beasts to true reason. Hence, even this very thing that I seem to have received for the adornment of the house, may it not impede my salvation, may its safety be dissipated. For I believe, and this is my faith, that from all these things which the law of Christianity abominates and prohibits, if I separate myself completely from them, I may deserve to attain present salvation and future.

58. Hearing these things, his son Tiburtius said: I will not allow this precious and principal and incomparable work to be cast down for any reason. But lest I

seem to come contrary to my father's salvation, let two ovens be brought and prepared, and let them be lit before the door of the chamber, so that when they have been destroyed by them, and my father has not received healing, both may be plunged into each of the burning ovens. Hearing this, his father forbade it to be done. But the saints not only did not fear the promised destruction, but also encouraged the preparation of the ovens with firmness.

59. Then the crystalline and glass idols and all that mechanical work approached: and suddenly, while they were being broken by the hands of the saints, a youth appeared before the eyes of Chromatius, whose face shone with a fiery radiance and said to him: My Lord Jesus Christ, in whom you have believed, has sent me to you, that you may receive healing of all your members. At this voice, the most healthy one restored began to run after the youth, to kiss his feet. But he said to him: See that you do not touch me, for the sanctification of baptism has not yet washed you from the filth of idols. Seeing this, Tiburtius his son rushed to the feet of St. Polycarp. But Chromatius the prefect was holding the feet of St. Sebastian, and both cried out with one voice: Christ is the true God, the only begotten Son of God, true and omnipotent, whom you good ministers proclaim.

CHAPTER XVII. The baptism of Chromatius and Tiburtius.

60. Then B. Sebastian said to Chromatius: As you know, I hold the command of the first cohort, but I have long decided not to know whether it is the militia of man, nor would I wish to. For this reason, I only wanted to hide under the cloak, to instruct the wavering spirits and to make the doubting steadfast, so that they would not yield to the pains of passions, whose faith had made warriors. But you, bearing the peak of the most ample power, cannot withdraw yourself from spectacles, nor can you be absent from judging affairs. Therefore,

feigning illness, I ask you to seek a successor for yourself, so that you may be free from the occupations of the world and take up the rudiments of future life, so that, born again by a second birth, you may become the offspring of eternal parents. Thus, on the same day, he sent to his friends placed in the palace, through whom, receiving testimonial writings, he accepted the initiation into divine military service before he was baptized.

61. What should I mention about how full of faith he was, and how sharp his intellect stood against the assertions of the infidels? The following reading makes it clear. For at the beginning, how the wave of the most sacred font was poured, the faith of his mind shone forth clearly. When asked if he believed, he said: I believe. When asked again whether he renounced all idols, he replied: I renounce. The priest's questioning continued, whether he renounced all sins; but he said: You should have inquired about this before I entered these halls of the King of Heaven. But now I wish to be re-inducted unbaptized, so that I may first forgive all those to whom I am angry; I will restore all my debtors their promissory notes; if I have violently taken anything from anyone, I will command it to be returned intact: I have two concubines after my wife's death, and I will grant them a dowry and hand them over to their husbands, I will free myself from all servile, freeborn, private, or public bonds of my actions: and then at last I promise to renounce all diabolical sins and pleasures of the world. Polycarp the priest said to him: You will be blessed by the heavenly wave, when you have completed with all haste what you say you will do: for the time of Lent is imposed on those to be baptized, so that for so many days they may learn to renounce all the arts of the enemy and the commerce of the world, if anyone truly wishes to become a Christian.

62. Then the wisest young man Tiburtius said: Father, if you demand time from me to renounce worldly affairs, I who was about to take up the affairs of

the forum, I renounce solely the will of acceptance: and I who was to be an advocate for the causes of mortals, I will take up Christianity, to engage in angelic actions, when I have begun to be one of those who receive eternal life and become advocates of holiness. Then Blessed Sebastian embraced him: and when he was baptized by S. Polycarp, he became the father of his acceptance.

63. Therefore, when only a few days had passed, and all had duly renounced the affairs of the world by Chromatius, Chromatius accepted the novelty of sacred baptism; and with him from his family, fourteen hundred souls of both sexes, whom he first freed from the bondage of servitude by the grace of manumission, and equipped with the best gifts, saying this: Those who begin to have God as their Father ought not to be the servants of man.

CHAPTER XVIII. Chromatius, having abdicated the prefecture of the City, nourishes Christians during the time of persecution.

64. Now there was a pope of the city of Rome named Caius, a man of great prudence and great virtue, during the reigns of Carinus, Diocletian, and Maximian. But Diocletian was in the City with Maximian; however, Carinus was with the whole army stationed in the regions of Gaul: and because of him, a slow persecution of Diocletian against Christians had begun; because Carinus had some friends whom the profession of this title adorned.

65. Therefore, after Carinus was killed in the city of Mainz by the consuls Maximian and Aquilinus, a persecution arose such that no one would buy or sell anything unless they had offered incense at the little altars set up in the place where they had come to buy. Around the islands, around the streets, even around the nymphaea, there were placed enforcers, who would neither allow

the opportunity to buy nor grant the very ability to draw water, unless they had offered it to the idols.

66. Then, having had a counsel of St. Caius the bishop, Chromatius, a distinguished man, received all Christians into his house, and he nurtured them all in such a way that no one at all would succumb to the necessity of sacrificing. But because such a force of persecution had arisen that the very opinion of Christianity could not be concealed, Chromatius deserved, by a sacred rescript, to remain for the sake of healing on the Campanian shore, where there was the lord of the broad turf, and he granted permission for any Christian who wished to go with him to avoid the rage of the persecutor. Then a contention arose between St. Polycarp and B. Sebastian; which of the two would remain in the city, and who would go with Chromatius, who had received such a Christian people. While they were arguing, the venerable pope Caius said: While both of you seek the crown of passion, you leave the acquired people of the Lord desolate. Therefore, it seems to me that you, brother Polycarp, since you hold the right path of the priesthood and are filled with the knowledge of God, should go together to strengthen the minds of the believers and to build up the wavering spirits. When he heard this, he was quiet and bore the gentle command of the pope with equanimity. And so the day of the Lord came, on which Bishop Caius, performing the things of God within the house of Chromatius, addressed all with this voice: Our Lord Jesus Christ, knowing the fragility of humanity, established two degrees in those believing in him, namely confession and martyrdom, so that those who despair of being able to bear the weight of martyrdom may hold onto the grace of confession, and giving their side to the soldiers of Christ, who are about to fight for his name, may bear concern. Therefore, let those who wish go together with our sons Chromatius and Tiburtius, and let those who wish remain with me in this city. For we are not divided by the spaces of the earth, whom the love of Christ

binds, nor do our eyes feel your absence, because we behold you with the gaze of the inner man.

67. While Pope Caius was speaking these and similar things, Tiburtius, a very distinguished man, exclaimed: I beseech you, father and bishop of bishops, do not allow me to give my back to those who pursue me. For it is very pleasing and desirable to me, if I could be killed a thousand times for the true God, so that I might find the dignity of that life, which no successor may take from me, to which no time may impose an end. Then St. Caius, rejoicing in his faith, shed tears, praying that all who remained would be victorious in the contest, receiving the triumph of martyrdom.

CHAPTER XIX. The illustrious deeds of Saints Sebastian, Tiburtius, and others in the City.

68. However, those who remained with the venerable Pope Caius were Marcellianus and Marcus, as well as their father, the most distinguished man Tranquillinus, also Blessed Sebastian, and the most beautiful youth, but also more beautiful in mind, St. Tiburtius, and Nicostratus from the first choir with his brother Castorius, and with his spouse, named Zoe; likewise Claudius with his brother Victorinus and with his son Symphorian, who had been freed from the disease of dropsy. These alone remained with Bishop Caius, while all others were departing with Chromatius: he sanctified Marcum and Marcellianum with the honor of deaconship but made their father Tranquillinus a priest. However, St. Sebastian, who lay hidden under the guise of a soldier for the benefit of many, he appointed as the defender of the Church, while he made the others subdeacons.

69. But because no safe place could be found for a hiding place, all stayed at a certain Christian named Castulus, a steward of the palace: who Castulus dwelt there in the palace, in a higher and very lofty place. This dwelling was deemed suitable because Castulus himself was most Christian with all his household; and the law given concerning sacrifices raged everywhere with its fervor against those who adhered to the palace, since there could be no suspicion against them, it was hidden. Therefore, as we said, all these were dwelling with holy Pope Caius at Castulus the steward, in the upper parts of the palace, and day and night occupied with groans and tears, and fasts and prayers, they implored the Lord, that they might be deemed worthy to be associated in the number of the holy martyrs by the endurance of his confession.

70. Meanwhile, while these things were happening, Blessed Tiburtius encountered a man who had fallen from a height, and had shaken his head and all his limbs, to such an extent that these were speaking only of his burial, of whom he was deemed worthy to be a son. Then he said to them weeping: Allow me to pray for him, perhaps he will recover his health. And when they all had given space, he approached him, and slowly saying the Lord's Prayer and the creed over his wounds, his bones were so solidified, and his head and all his entrails, that as if nothing had happened to him, he became whole.

71. Therefore, after he had done this, he began to go. However, his parents held him saying: Come and have him as a servant, and we entrust all our goods to you with him, because you have restored him alive to us, the only one we had, now dead. He says to them: If you do what I tell you, I will greatly value the reward of this health. His parents say to him: If you deign to have us as servants, we cannot oppose it: indeed, we even desire it, if you judge it worthy. Then taking their hands, he separated them from the crowds and showed them the power of the name of Christ. And seeing their minds firmly fixed in the fear of

the Lord, he led them to Pope Caius and said: Venerable pope and chief of the divine law, behold whom Christ has gained through me today, in whom my faith covers the young sprout, which first burst forth into fruit. Then St. Caius the bishop baptized them, that is, the youth with his parents, giving thanks to God.

CHAPTER XX. The martyrdom of Saints Zoe, Tranquillinus, and others.

73. But because it is much if we wish to pursue what and how great things Christ has done through them, let us merely explain how each one came to the palm of martyrdom. The most blessed Zoe, while praying at the birth of the Apostles for the confession of the Apostle Peter, was constrained by lurking pagans, and was led to the patron of the region Naumachiae and was compelled to burn drops of incense to the statue of Mars, which stood there. Then she responded: You compel a woman to sacrifice to Mars, to show that your Mars delights in women. But he, being able to take away modesty from the most impudent Venus, will not prevail against me who bears the trophy of faith on my forehead. For I do not struggle against him with my own strength; but trusting in the power of my Lord Jesus Christ, I scorn both you and him together with laughter. Then the patron of the region sent her into the most obscure custody, and for five days made her neither see light, nor receive food or drink. Only the voice of him who had enclosed her there was heard saying: You will die there of hunger, thirst, and blindness, unless you promise to libate to the gods.

74. But when six days had passed, they suggested to the raging prefect about her: who ordered her to be suspended from a high tree by her neck and hair and to be subjected to smoke from dung. Immediately as she was suspended, she emitted her spirit in the confession of the Lord. But they, taking away her body,

bound it with a stone and immersed it in the Tiber, saying: Let not Christians take away her body, and make her a goddess for themselves.

75. Therefore, after her martyrdom was celebrated, Blessed Sebastian came to her in a dream and told him how she had received the martyrdom of the Lord. When he had narrated this, St. Sebastian was stirred, saying: Women precede to the crown, why do we live? He also, descending on the eighth day of the birth of the Apostles, approached the confession of Blessed Paul: nonetheless, he himself suffered ambushes and was stoned to death by the people, and his body was entrusted to the Tiberine whirlpool.

76. Nicostratus and Claudius, along with Castorius, Victorinus, and Symphorian, while they were seeking the bodies of the Saints through the Tiber, were captured by persecutors and brought before the prefect of the City. The judge was Fabian, who urged them to sacrifice, and for ten days, by threats and flattery, he could not move them at all. Then he made a suggestion to the emperors, who ordered that they be tormented until the third time. And when they yielded to no torture, he ordered them to be thrown into the sea. Thus, constrained by immense weights, they were cast into the waves of the sea, and in a pure place among the waters, they celebrated the crown of martyrdom. Therefore, the unfaithful lay in wait for the faithful, and tormented by wicked fury, they could not even bear to hear the name of a Christian.

CHAPTER XXI. The Martyrdom of St. Tiburtius.

77. Meanwhile, while a certain individual had associated himself with St. Caius the bishop under a feigned faith, claiming to be a Christian; furthermore, this man had been an apostate and was deceitful in all his speech, and cunning in all his dealings. To make a long story short, while he was frequently reproached by

Blessed Tiburtius, a most learned, noble, and holy man, for arranging his hair with the skill of a barber, for constantly indulging himself and playing during meals; for giving himself more freely to the gaze of women, and for withdrawing from fasts and prayers, that he did not attend vigilantly to the hymns of God through the nights; while for these things, as we said, he was sharply reproached by Blessed Tiburtius, he pretended to accept the admonition calmly: and he cleverly acted so that the unfaithful would seize praying St. Tiburtius. In this capture, he made it appear that he himself was being held, and at the same time was led to the secretarium of the raging judge. But when they were brought in, Fabian the prefect said to him, who had surrendered himself by trickery: "What do you say?" And he answered: "Torquatus." Fabian said: "What do you profess?" Torquatus said: "I am a Christian." Fabian said: "Do you not know what the invincible princes have ordered, that those who do not wish to sacrifice to the gods be tormented by various tortures?" Torquatus said: "This is my master, and he has always taught me: what I see him do, it is necessary for me to do."

78. Fabian turned to St. Tiburtius and said: "Have you heard what Torquatus asserts? How do you respond to these things?" St. Tiburtius said: "Torquatus has long pretended to be a Christian; for the virtue of the holy name itself bears heavily and painfully, that his name is not usurped by his lovers. Truly, the most illustrious man, this Christian name is of divine virtue, of the followers of Christ, who have truly philosophized, who have truly been called Christians, who have fought bravely to overcome lusts. Do you believe, most illustrious man, that he is a Christian, who commits fringes to the grinding of his head in lechery, who loves the barber, who carries his shoulders softly, who stretches his gait with wicked effort, who treats men carelessly, and gazes more attentively at women? Christ has never deemed such as worthy to have servants. But since he

claims that he will imitate me here, you will prove in your presence that he is lying. For he will now evidently show what he has always been."

79. Fabian said: "You will do more wisely if you consider your own safety and do not despise the decrees of the princes." St. Tiburtius said: "I do not better consult my safety than to despise the gods and goddesses and confess that my one Lord Jesus Christ is my God." Torquatus said: "Not only is he cruelly a Christian, but he also persuades many, deceives, and teaches that all the gods are demons; he, however, with his companions, with whom he practices magical arts, is occupied day and night with incantations." St. Tiburtius said: "A false witness will not be unpunished." And he said to the judge: "This one, whom you see, most illustrious man, seething with the cares of his wickedness, is joined to nothing else but to consider how he might present himself to us as a Christian; how he might lie to others that he is most faithful. Yet I reproached him for Cyclopean gluttony, and for shame drowned in wine, and for the sanctity of the divine name buried. Drunken, he suffered thirst and hunger, vomiting: nor as a Christian, but as an Antonian, he eats, drinks, vomits, and now accuses Christians, incites a mild judge against us, offers a sword to the unwilling judge, and urges us to bow our necks to demons. We see your vow, we see your bloody plans; and we behold the wicked art of words, the poison of your heart. Now prepare yourself most cruelly: use the office of the executioner: avenge yourself and the voice of the judge; apply the stings, hang the Christians, inflict, strike, burn, apply all tortures; you have received us well. If you threaten exile, the whole world is for philosophers; if punishment, we escape the prison of the world; if fires, we conquer greater things in these desires. Decide whatever you wish, every penalty is worthless to us where pure conscience is our companion."

80. The prefect Fabian said: "Restore yourself to your kind and be what nature has dictated to you. For being born noble, you have fallen into such filth, that you wish to undergo both punishment and infamy and death at the same time." St. Tiburtius said: "O most prudent of men, and judge appointed by the Romans! because I do not wish to worship Venus the harlot, and incestuous Jupiter, and deceitful Mercury, and Saturn the slayer of children, I incur the infamy of nobility: and because I adore and revere the one and true God, who reigns in heaven, you threaten that I should be tormented. We do not agree with your persuasion: we do not deny; that Christ the Son of God descended from heaven to earth, so that from the earth man might ascend to heaven; therefore, I trample underfoot all these vain images, which you worship without cause, and I subject myself to Almighty God.

81. Then Fabian ordered burning coals to be poured out before his feet; and he said to him: Choose for yourself one of two, either add incense to these coals, or walk barefoot upon them. Then Blessed Tiburtius, making the sign of the cross, boldly stepped upon them with bare feet, and began to say to the prefect: Lay aside your unbelief and learn that here alone is God, whom we confess to reign over all creatures. Send forth your hand, if you can, in the name of your god Jupiter into hot water; and if your Jupiter can, let him make you not feel the heat of the flames. For me, in the name of my Lord Jesus Christ, it seems that I walk upon rose-colored flowers, because the creature serves the command of its Creator.

82. Fabian said: Who does not know that you have taught your Christ magic? St. Tiburtius said: Be silent, wretched one, and do not do me this injury with your ears, as to hear you barking with a rabid mouth, naming his sweet name as holy. Then an angry Fabian dictated the sentence saying: Let the blasphemer of the gods, and the one guilty of atrocious injuries, be punished with the sword.

He was led to the Lavican way, three miles from the City, and pouring forth a prayer to the Lord, he was struck down by a single blow of the sword. And in that same place he was buried by a certain Christian parent: in which place Christ has always bestowed many benefits to the praise of his name even to the present day.

CHAPTER XXII. The Martyrdom of Saints Castulus, Marcellianus, and Marcus.

83. After these things, Torquatus acted so that Castulus the servant of the palace, host of the Saints, might be captured: who, when he had been pressed, and was hung up for the third time, having been heard for the third time, persevering in the confession of the Lord, was sent into a pit and a mass of sand was poured upon him, and he departed to the Lord with the palm of martyrdom.

84. After this, Marcellianus and Marcus were held; and both bound to a stake received sharp nails in their feet; to whom the most insane Fabian said: You will stand fixed on your feet until you repay the due service to the gods. Then both brothers, being fixed to one piece of wood, sang saying: Behold how good and how pleasant it is for brothers to dwell together in unity. Fabian said to them: Unfortunate and miserable ones, lay aside your madness, and free yourselves from the impending tortures upon you. To whom both responded: Never have we feasted so well: now we have begun to be fixed in the love of Christ. Would that you permit us to be as we are for as long as we are clothed with this garment of the body. And when one day and one night had passed, and they persevered in psalms and hymns, he ordered both of them, where they stood, to be struck with spears through their sides: and thus, through the glory of martyrdom, they migrated to the starry kingdoms. They too were buried on the

Appian way, two miles from the City, in a place called Ad Arenas, because there were crypts of sand from which the walls of the City were built.

CHAPTER XXIII. The Glorious Contest of St. Sebastian.

85. With these things having been done, Blessed Sebastian was encountered by those lying in wait: and because, as we said, he seemed to be hiding under a cloak, when he was a most worthy soldier of Christ, the prefect suggested about him to Emperor Diocletian. Who, calling him to himself, said: I have always held you among the first of my palace. And you have hitherto hidden against my safety to the injury of the gods. St. Sebastian said: For your safety I have always worshiped Christ, and for the state of the Roman world, I have always adored him, who is in heaven, considering that to seek help from stones is the act of a mad head and vain. Then Diocletian, enraged, ordered him to be led into the middle of the field, and to be bound as a target for arrows, and commanded that archers should shoot him. Then the soldiers placed him in the middle of the field and filled him with arrows from both sides, so that he was as if he were covered with the quills of a hedgehog from the strikes of the arrows.

86. But estimating him to be dead, they went away. Then, leaving the martyr Castulus the servant, a woman named Irene, very devout, went by night to take and bury his body. And finding him alive, she brought him to her home on a high staircase where she stayed near the palace, and there within a few days he recovered perfect health in all his limbs.

87. And when all the Christians gathered to him, they urged him to depart. But he, having made a prayer, descended, and standing on the steps of Heliogabalus, said to the approaching emperors: By wicked subterfuges, the souls of your empire are besieged by the pontiffs of the temples, suggesting false

tales about Christians, saying they are adversaries of the Republic; whose prayers improve and increase the Republic itself; who do not cease to pray for your empire and for the safety of the Roman army. When he was saying these things and such, Diocletian said: Are you Sebastian, whom we ordered to be killed with arrows some time ago? St. Sebastian said: The Lord Jesus Christ has deemed me worthy to be resurrected for this purpose, that I might meet and testify to you before all the people, that your unjust judgment has burst forth against the servants of Christ.

88. Then he ordered him to be led into the hippodrome of the palace, and to be beaten until he breathed his last. Then they took his body by night and sent it into the Cloaca Maxima, saying: lest perhaps Christians make him a martyr for themselves. Then Blessed Sebastian appeared in a dream to St. Lucina, a certain very devout matron, saying: In that sewer, which is near the circus, you will find my body hanging in a gromphus. This you, when you have lifted it, will carry it to the catacombs and bury it at the beginning of the crypt next to the footsteps of the Apostles.

89. Then Blessed Lucina herself went by herself with her servants in the middle of the night, and lifting him, she placed him in her peacock, and led him to the place where he had commanded, and buried him with all diligence. But the holy Lucina did not depart from that holy place for thirty days.

90. After some years, peace was restored to the Church: which as soon as the Church received the glory of peace, made her house a church. To which, leaving all her wealth for the rest of Christians, she made the Church herself an heir in Christ, who lives and reigns equal with God the Father and the Holy Spirit in the unity of virtue, forever and ever. Amen.

LATIN TEXT

CAPUT PRIMUM. S. Sebastianus martyres animat.

1. Sebastianus vir christianissimus Mediolanensium partibus eruditus civis vero Narbonensis, Diocletiano et Maximiano imperatoribus ita charus erat, ut principatum ei primae cohortis traderent, et suo eum conspectui juberent semper astare. Erat enim vir totius prudentiae, in sermone verax, in judicio justus, in consilio providus, in commisso fidelis, in interventu strenuus, in bonitate conspicuus, in universa morum honestate praeclarus. Hunc milites ac si patrem venerabantur; hunc universi, qui praeerant palatio, charissimo venerabantur affectu: erat enim verus Dei cultor, et necesse erat ut, quem Dei perfuderat gratia, ab omnibus amaretur.

2. Christo igitur quotidie sedulum exhibebat officium, sed agebat quatenus hoc sacrilegis regibus esset occultum, non passionis timore perterritus, nec patrimonii sui amore constrictus, sed ad hoc tantum sub chlamyde terreni imperii Christi militem agebat absconditum, ut Christianorum animos, quos inter tormenta videbat deficere, confortaret, et Deo redderet animas quas diabolus conabatur auferre.

3. Denique postquam multas martyrum mentes a timore passionis eripuit, et ad coronam perpetuae gloriae incitavit: ipse quis esset, apparuit, quia lumen in tenebris latere non potuit. Clarissimis igitur viris Marcelliano et Marco duobus geminis fratribus pro Christi nomine in vinculis constitutis, quotidie solatium exhibebat; et tam ipsis quam etiam servis eorum, cum quibus tenti fuerant, salutaria fidei consilia ministrabat: quibus fugitiva saeculi blandimenta respuerent, et momentanea tormentorum genera non timerent.

CAPUT II. Marcelliani et Marci graviter oppugnata constantia.

4. Qui cum beatissimis consolationibus acquiescerent, et verbera carnificum animo perseveranti transirent, capitalem jussi sunt subire sententiam: ea videlicet ratione, ut si eodem momento quo decollandi erant sacrificiis consensissent, et parentibus suis et conjugibus et filiis et facultatibus redderentur. Erant enim non solum, ut diximus, genere clarissimi viri, sed et facultatibus dilatati; quorum erat pater Tranquillinus nomine, et mater Marcia vocabatur; qui illos sequebantur cum uxoribus eorum et filiis; nimio enim in suis nepotibus ducebantur affectu. Unde factum est, ub ab Agrestio Chromatio urbis Romae praefecto triginta dierum inducias impetrarent, in quorum spatio ageretur cum eis, quatenus ad thurificandum idolis consentirent.

5. Accedentes itaque amici eorum ad eos, coeperunt dicere: Unde vobis tam dura mens, tamque ferreum pectus, quod canitiem patimini patris abjicere, et matri jam decrepitae novos dolores partus afferre? Nam illa partus sui dolores consolationibus superabat, dum in uno dolore duos filios pareret, et geminum patri funderet filiorum affectum: nunc vero insanabilis dolor, inconsolabilis poena, irremediabilis cruciatus, incomparabilis partus est, quo spes et gaudium tollitur, vita contemnitur, respuitur gloria, et, contemptis omnibus pietatis affectibus, mortis atrocitas appetitur potiusquam timetur. Obsecramus vos, o amici charissimi, tandem his date cladibus finem, et vos patres esse dulcium filiorum vel admoniti mementote.

6. Haec et his similia amici dicentibus, miseram se clamitans mater advenit, et soluto capite canos suae senectutis ostentans, in conspectu eorum vestem qua pectus tegebatur, scidit: et cunctis flentibus ostendebat eis laxis pellibus quas suxerant mammas, et blandimenta, quae infantiae eorum exhibuerat, ejulando

lacrymans memorabat. Aiebat ergo ad ambos: Tu mihi semper plus blanditus es, fili; et tu amplius verecundatus es: in isto imaginem meam peperi, in te paternos vultus effudi; tu patri utilior, iste similior. Heu me miseram! circumvallant me ex omni parte incomparabiles luctus, inaudita miseria et gemina orbitas, nullis penitus tribulationibus comparanda. Omitto filios ad mortem ultro properantes, quos si mihi hostes auferrent, per medias sequerer acies bellatorum; si judicia violenta concluderent, carcerem simul irrumperem moritura. Novum hoc genus est pereundi, in quo carnifex rogatur ut feriat, vita optatur ut pereat, mors invitatur ut veniat. Novus hic luctus est; nova miseria, in qua natorum juventus sponte amittitur, et parentum miseranda cogitur senectus ut vivat.

7. Ista et his similia matre prosequente, infirmus pater, et gravis jam senio, manibus adducitur servulorum, et cygnaeo capiti terrae pulverem spargens, hujusmodi dabat voces ad coelum: Ad mortem ultro proficiscentibus filiis valedicturus adveni, ut universa, quae a filiis sepulturae meae exhibenda paraveram, ego infelix filios sepulturus expendam. O filii, meae baculus senectutis, et geminum meorum viscerum lumen, nati feliciter, et prospere educati, excellentissimae memoriae, et ingenii singularis, omnium liberalium peritia litterarum imbuti, quae ista repente insania vestra voluntate progenita mortis vos fecit esse amatores? Numquam ista viventibus placuit: numquam morituris suum amorem induxit: ad quoscumque autem pervenire potuit, violenter admissa est, et non est voluntate ab ullo vivente suscepta. Si hanc nudus debitor sub avaro feneratore patitur, nulla potest ratione diligere; nec solum non diligere cognoscitur, sed timere. Qua ratione eam appetit, qui et bonis exuberat omnibus, et penitus ulli nihil debet? Venite huc, senes, et mecum super filios plangite, qui vos viscera paterna habere sentitis. Venite huc, juvenes, et flete super juvenes sponte pereuntes. Huc accedite, patres, et prohibete talia, ne talia patiamini. Deficite plorando, oculi mei, et caliginem

obducite fundentes flumina lacrymarum; ne videam caedi gladio, quos dum virga levis tangeret, tremui; dum tristantes leviter viderem, expavi.

8. Igitur dum haec et alia senior prosequeretur, ecce amborum conjuges cum natis propriis veniunt, et aspectibus eorum proprios infantulos offerentes, has ejulando voces effundunt: Quibus nos servituras relinquitis? quibus conjugii nostri traditis charitatem? qui putatis erunt horum infantium domini, et domorum vestrarum avidissimi pervasores? Qui erunt vestrae occupatores familiae? vel qui sibi divisuri sunt vernaculos, quos nutristis? Heu quam ferreo, heu quam impiae crudelitatis genere parentes despicitis, amicos respuitis, uxores abjicitis, filios abdicatis, et vos ipsos carnifici ultroneos exhibetis!

CAPUT III. S. Sebastianus nutantes confirmat.

9. Interea dum illa dicuntur, et ista referuntur, inter uxorum lacrymas, et suspiria filiorum, coeperunt milites Christi mollescere, et animos suos flectere ad dolorem. Huic spectaculo, ut supra diximus, intererat S. Sebastianus, vir per omnia christianissimus, quem occultabat militaris habitus, et chlamydis obumbrabat aspectus. At ubi vidit athletas Dei immenso certaminis pondere fatigari, in medio eorum se objiciens, dixit: O fortissimi milites Christi, o instructissimi divini praelii bellatores, per nimiam virtutem animi fortiter pervenistis ad palmam, et nunc per misera blandimenta coronam deponitis sempiternam? Discat nunc per vos Christi militum fortitudo, fide potius armari quam ferro. Nolite victoriarum vestrarum insignia per mulierum blandimenta abjicere, et subjectas pedibus vestris hostis devicti cervices ad victricia et rediviva iterum bella laxare, cujus quamvis saeva contra vos extiterit et periniqua instantia, saevior tamen efficitur ira repetita. Erigite igitur a terrenis affectibus tropaeum vestri certaminis gloriosum, et nolite illud amittere fletibus parvulorum.

10. Isti, quos plorantes attenditis, gauderent hodie si possent scire quae nostis; putant enim quod ista vita sit sola, quae si finem acceperit, nulla vitalis animae, corpore deficiente, valeat portio remanere. Si enim scirent esse alteram vitam ignaram mortis, tristitiae nesciam, in qua immortalitas regnat, et perpetua gaudia commorantur; profecto vobiscum ad illam festinarent pertingere, et vitam illam pro nihilo computantes, illam appeterent, quae et in exsultatione permanet et penitus finiri non novit. Ista enim vita fugitiva est et tam infideils, ut nec amatoribus suis fidem potuerit custodire. Ab origine enim mundi in se credentes fefellit, omnes se exspectantes decepit, cunctos de se praesumentes irrisit, et ita nullum omnino certum reddidit, ut omnibus probetur fuisse mentita. Atque utinam solius mendacii culpae esset obnoxia, et per omnia crimina currere suos non cogeret amatores. Ipsa dat edacitatem glutonibus, ipsa ebrietatem ingerit temulentis, ipsa naufragium pudoris adulteris, ipsa exsecrabilem tradit perversitatem incestis; ipsa admonet furem, ut rapiat; iracundum, ut saeviat; mendacem, ut fallat. Ipsa inter conjuges divortia seminat, inter amicos discordias, inter pacificos lites, inter justos injustitiam, inter fratres scandala. Ipsa tollit judicibus justitiam, castis pudicitiam, artificibus peritiam, ipsa aufert moribus disciplinam. Et ut altiora quae amatoribus suis ingerit crimina memoremus; si fratrem aliquando frater germanus occidit, si filius necavit patrem, si interemptus est ab amico amicus; cujus haec instinctu facta sunt scelera, cujus intuitu, cujus spe, cujus fiducia ista sunt nefanda commissa? Numquid non praesentis vitae amore seducti ista committunt, et dum illam plusquam justum est diligunt, iniquo odio homines prosequuntur? Ut quid enim pirata navigantem jugulat, ut quid latro perimit viatorem, dives opprimit pauperem, superbus humilem, et omnis nocens quemcumque potuerit aggravat innocentem? Haec autem faciunt mala, quia isti vitae servire desiderant, et se existimant in amore ejus per tempora prolixiora durare. Non ergo alterius causa fiunt scelera nisi ut infelicissimae isti carnali vitae a carnalibus serviatur.

11. Ipsa est denique quae eis crimina imperat, jubet facinora, suadet injusta; et posteaquam omni crudelitate, omnique fuerit spurcitia saginata, servientes sibi tradit filiae suae, id est morti perpetuae. Ex ipsa enim, et ex ejus utero mors aeterna est nata, tempore quo gulae suae et libidini et delectationibus oculorum primi homines servierunt; atque ideo qui ad aeternam vitam facti fuerant, huc in istam sunt regionem mortis jactati: hinc iterum sunt ad inferos devoluti, nihil secum praeter peccata portantes. Haec ergo vita est quae vos fallit, o amici charissimi, ut amicos vestros ad vitam euntes perpetuam injusto consilio revocetis.

CAPUT IV. Inferni poenae, coelique gaudia, martyrum aninis inculcata.

12. Haec vos instigat, o parentes sanctissimi, ut filios vestros proficiscentes ad comitatum coeli, ad honorem incorruptibilem, ad amicitias imperatoris aeterni, stultissimis lamentationibus revocetis. Ista est quae vos, o castissimae conjuges Beatorum, per pietatis colorem impietatem Martyrum mentibus fecit tradere, et necem pro liberatione afferre. Si enim consensissent revocationi vestrae, pauco quidem tempore vobiscum esse poterant; postea vero separari, et ita habuerant separari a vobis, ut numquam vos nisi inter tormenta perpetua videretis; ubi edax flamma incredulorum animas devorat, ubi dracones blasphemantium labia comedunt, ubi serpentes morsibus suis incredulorum pectora depascuntur. Illic ululatus et gemitus sonat, et clamor confusus, quem vis tormentorum exagitat, et incendii arsura extorquet. Haec ipsa autem tribulatio, quae illic excipiet infideles, nullo termino definitur, nullo fine concluditur, sed nec post flammarum atrocium adustionem consumitur, sed ad rediviva incendia iterum qui adustus fuerit reparatur.

13. Hanc ergo poenam et istos permittite evadere, et vosmetipsos eripere cogitate. Permittite interim istos ad coronam pertingere destinatam. Nolite

timere; non enim separabuntur a vobis, sed vadent praeparare vobis in coelo sidereas mansiones, in quibus una vobiscum et cum filiis vestris in perpetuo gaudio maneatis. Quod si vos domus vestrae ex lapidibus factae delectant; quanto magis illarum vos debet pulchritudo invitare domorum ubi sunt triclinia auro puro radiantia, quae ex gemmis et margaritis habent zetas instructas? Illic flos purpureus rosarum numquam marcessit: illic florida nemora perpetua viriditate vernant: illic prata recentia semper melleis fluunt rivis: illic croceis gramina floribus redolent, et halantes campi jucundis admodum odoribus pollent. Aurae ibi vitam aeternam habentes naribus nectareum odorem aspirant. Lumen ibi sine solis radio fulgens, serenitas absque nubilo, et absque tenebris nocturnis die oculi perfruuntur. Nulla illic impediuntur occupatione deliciae, nulla penitus sollicitudine ibi securitas conturbatur; mugitus, ululatus, gemitus, lamentum et luctus numquam illic audita nec nominata sunt: foedum et deforme, tetrum, nigrum, horrendum aliquid, aut sordidum numquam ibi penitus viderunt oculi habitantium: pulchritudine vero in amaenitate nemorum, splendore in aere jocundo et formositate atque omni elegantia sine intermissione oculi patentes perfruuntur; et nihil omnino quod conturbet mentem auribus datur. Sonant enim ibi jugiter organa hymnorum, quae ad laudem regis ab angelis et archangelis decantantur. Amaritudo et fellis asperitas ibi locum non habent: tonitrua ibi numquam audita sunt, fulgura et coruscationes numquam paruerunt. Cinnamomum illic virgulta gignunt, et balsamum arbusta prorumpunt. Odor aeris delectationem per omnia membra diffundit, et esca ibi nulla stercora conficit. Sicut enim bono nuntio aures, et bono odore nares, et bono aspectu oculi saginantur, et ista refectio non potest in digestionem prorumpere; ita illic refectio, quam os susceperit, melliflua in gustu hoc unicuique sapit, quo fuerit delectatus. Statim denique quod concupierit anima, desiderio ejus universa famulantur, et omnibus delectationibus ejus paratissimus servit effectus.

14. Nam qui in ista mortali vita, contra concupiscentias suas et contra delectationes pugnaverit, quisquis eas hic non expenderit, illic eas integras a suo Creatore consequitur. Ipse enim ita creavit hominem ut viveret: et mortem juxta introitum delectationis posuit, ut hi queis libet a mortis timore evadere, vitam aeternam quaerant; et dum praeter istam vitam alteram esse didicerint, inquirant utrum et ipsa possit senectute intercidi aut morte concludi: quam dum immortalem agnoverint, inquirant utrum possit iterum ipsa aeternitas vel honorem tradere justis vel injustis poenam inferre.

CAPUT V. Opum deliciarumque usus.

15. Cumque specialiter ita esse probaverint, restat, ut interrogent, cur a Creatore divitiae factae sint, si ejus lege contemnendae sunt, vel quare quadrupedum et volucrum atque repentium varietas a Creatore facta sit, si singulis renuntiandum est: cur autem ab ipso Creatore medullitus genuina delectatio ad incitamentum est libidinis fundata corporibus, si usus ejus auctori non solum eum faciat reum, sed etiam perpetuis tradat incendiis. Interrogatur ergo: Cur a Creatore divitiae datae sunt, si contemnendae sunt? Respondemus: Istae divitiae a Creatore factae, alloquuntur quodammodo amatores suos, dicentes: Sic nos amate, ut a vobis numquam separemus. Sequi vos morientes non possumus; antecedere autem vos viventes possumus; sed si ipsi jubeatis. Cupidus foenerator et avarus agricola, unus aurum tradit homini quod duplicatum recipiat, alius diversa semina terrae committit, ut si possit fieri quod simplem tradit centuplum quaerat recipere: et debitor aurum creditori reddit duplicatum, et terra semen reddit centuplicatum. Proh nefas! fenus debitor feneratori reddere praevalet; et terra agricolae suo restituere centuplicata semina potest; Deus divitias suas si a te acceperit, eas tibi amplificatas reddere non potest?

16. Inquiris nunc: Cur divitias mihi dedit, si a me ipsi reddendae sunt? Tradidit eas tibi, ut scias quanta sit in eis requies, quanta voluptas, quantus luxus, quantaeque possunt esse deliciae, ut per haec habens charitatem cum divitiis tuis, ipse eas tradas custodiendas Domino nostro Jesu Christo. Quas si ipsi nolueris credere, aut edacitas gulae eas invadet, aut luxuria libidinum mater tibi eas eripiet, aut sine dubio, quod nosti optime, mors ex improviso aggrediens ita tibi illas extorquet, ut tu illas ulterius in toto nec habere praevideas, nec videre. Numquid si transires per medias acies barbarorum, et invenires fortem virum qui te semper dilexit, qui tibi etiam sacculum pecuniis donaverat plenum, dicentem tibi: Da mihi custodiendas pecunias quas dedi tibi; quia isti barbari insidiantur ut eas tibi auferant, quas dum tibi abstulerint suis te gladiis laniabunt; numquid non pedibus ejus advolutus rogares eum, ut eas ipse susciperet, de quo certus esses quod et ampliora quam acceperat redderet, et te ipsum ab hostibus liberaret? Restat nunc ut divitiis vestris tutorem possitis habere Christum.

17. Ad delicias veniamus. Qui habet aures audiendi, audiet eas dicentes sibi: Si vere amatores nostri estis, illi nos commendate, qui nos vobis integras illibatasque in illa regione restituat, in qua vobiscum jugiter manere possimus: in ista enim vita si vobis nostrum voluerimus occupare servitium, quasi hic expertae, ibi vobis omnino negabimus nostrae, servitutis officium. Dimittite nos interim servire morituris, quia idcirco breviati sunt dies mortalibus, ut immortalibus jugiter famulemur. Sic enim scriptum est (Matth. XXIV, 22): Propter electos breviabuntur dies, ut servitus nostra non sit longa. Injustis quidem servimus festino cursu: impiis, sceleratis et turpibus servimus, non sponte; sed propter eum qui nos subdidit. Liberabimur tamen a servitute corruptionis, et revocabimur ad libertatem gloriae filiorum Dei. Omnis itaque delectatio, futurae vitae servata, non perditur; neque enim repositi thesauri

existimantur ab eo qui eos absconderat in terris, interesse; sed magis tanto securius se eos habere confidit, quanto eos occultius et tutius collocaverit.

18. Sint ergo repositae omnium deliciarum affluentiae, ut non contingantur in ista vita, quae praeterit: quia si hic in usu fuerint, in illa vita, quae numquam praeterit, amittentur. Esto, quod ista vita centum tendatur annorum spatiis, numquid exclusa die ultima non statim videbitur quasi non fuisse, et ac memoria hospitis uno die apud nos manentis vestigia reliquisse? Illa autem vita manet jugiter, et perseverat instanter, annis quoque labentibus juvenescit et pollet, et inde renovationis sumit initium unde finis accipitur. O vere illum degenerem et omnium bonorum expertem, qui hujus tam formosae vitae amore non capitur! qui timet istam vitam tradere perituram, et illam accipere quae penitus perire non novit, in qua deliciae et delectationes, et divitiae, et gaudia sic inchoant, ut terminum nesciant; sic principium capiunt, ut penitus finire non possint.

19. Nam qui hujus tam praeclarae vitae amator esse noluerit, non solum istam perdit, et ad illam non pervenit, verum etiam ut jam dixi a perpetua morte capitur et tenetur; in qua est jugis flamma, perseverans tribulatio, et poena perpetua; in qua atroces angeli commorantur, quorum brachia capita draconum sunt, quorum oculi ex se igneas sagittas jaculantur; quorum dentes sicut elephantis prominent, et stimulant ad tormentum veluti caudae scorpionum, quorum voces veluti leonum fremitus sonant, quorum aspectus tremorem incutit pariter et dolorem et mortem. Atque utinam mors posset in his angustiis constitutis occurrere! Sed quod est acerbius, ad hoc vivitur, ut cruciatibus gubernetur, ad hoc redintegrantur, ut exesa serpentium morsibus membra iteratis subinde et iterum repetitis morsibus attrectentur.

CAPUT VI. Martyrum felicitas et gloria.

20. Haec est omnis causa certaminis, quae poenas martyrii docet tolerabiler debere sufferri. Nolite ergo, o amici, nolite, o parentes, nolite, o conjuges venerandae sanctorum, nolite a vita ad mortem, quos diligitis revocare, a gaudio ad luctum ducere, a lumine ad tenebras trahere, et ab aeterna requie ad poenas sempiternas accersire. Hoc est cum diabolo quasi piscibus hamum tendere, et invitare ad modicam suavitatem, in qua intus lateat cruciatus viscerum, et mors interiorum tormentis extorta. Numquid non hoc est ad compensationem aeternarum deliciarum fugitiva gaudia anteponere; et ut perparum rideant, aeternis fletibus mancipare? Hoc in gladiatoribus, qui ultro se offerunt, universi damnamus, qui considerant unius anni delicias, et non considerant, qui fructus ex ipsis deliciis oriatur. Et illi cruciantur ictibus gladiorum, vel alterna coede interna viscerum, scisso ventris tegmine, in conspectu proferunt populorum, ut pinguedo, quam inconsulta sagina contulerat, offeratur diabolo devoranda. Isto consilio inimici, quo isti haec faciunt, ipso consilio ad vitam aeternam euntes Dei Martyres revocantur, qui ut vitam paucorum dierum vivant exorantur perpetuos cruciatus incurrere, et mortem perpetuam, quae specialiter metuenda est, non timere.

21. Huic loco forte illud apponitis: Quare Christianus tormenta non metuit, et praesentis non terretur poena tortoris? Ideo non frangitur metu, ideo dolore non ducitur, quia scit se unius doloris pretio perpetuae sanitatis gaudium emere; et per momentaneam tribulationem ad perpetuam felicitatem et sempiternam laetitiam pervenire. Sed si iste timendus sit dolor, timendus sit carnifex, timenda quoque sit nova et exquisita tortoris crudelitas; quae magis timenda, quae horrenda, quae magis fugienda est, et cavenda, ista quae hodie effervescit, et cras evanescit? ista quae hodie exardescit, et cras refrigescit? ista quae sub hora inducitur, et sub hora excluditur? an illa quae nullo fine

concluditur, nullo tempore exstinguitur, nulla prorsus consumitur vetustate? Nam iste dolor aut levis est, et potest tolerabiliter sustineri; aut gravis est, et glorioso certamine citatum offert finem; ille autem poenarum dolor et cruciatus incendii, qui hujus vitae amatoribus datur, cum sit vehementior universo tormentorum genere, numquam finiendus aggreditur, et acrius subinde quam inchoaverit saevit, et nullus saeviendi terminus, nullus omnino finis occurrit, sed habens secum universa suppliciorum genera subinde renovatur ut saeviat, augmentatur ut excruciet, inflammatur ut acrius urat.

22. Hinc ergo ab hoc interitu, quos amamus, hortemur evadere; et nos ipsos ad evadendum fortiter praeparemus: nec timeamus una hora ferre dolorem in corpore, qui optamus perpetuo gaudere cum Christo, permittamus animam nostram cum palma martyrii ex hoc egredi corpore, ut possimus poenas aeternas evadere, et ad possessiones sidereas plenas delectationibus pervenire. Lacrymas nostras convertamus in gaudium: quia non debemus quasi morituros plangere, quos cum Christo credimus regnaturos. Congratulemur victoribus hostium, conculcata eorum cervice: congaudeamus martyrii praetexta indutis, et coeli factos consules gloriemur. En dies in quo vincere se tyrannus existimabat, qui dum capit, captus est; dum tenet, vinctus est; dum torquet, tortus est: dum insultat, irrisus est; dum jugulat, occisus est. Nunc ergo in amore martyrii etiam nostros suscitemus affectus; ut illum qui de nostra captivitate voluit victoriam capere, fortiter capiamus, et quasi a gravi somno expergefacti aperiamus oculos animorum, ut videntes foveas quas in nostri perniciem inimicus aptaverat, nos quidem auxiliante Deo evadamus, et ipso diabolo cum satellitibus suis in ipsam quam paraverat foveam incidente, nos cum propheta dicamus: Foderunt ante faciem meam foveam, et ipsi inciderunt in eam (Psal. LVI, 7).

CAPUT VII. Sebastiani oratione et miraculis, consersi Zoe et Nicostratus.

23. Igitur cum haec beatissimus Sebastianus, indutus chlamyde, succinctus baltheo, ex suo ore proferret, subito per unam fere horam splendore nimio de coelo veniente illuminatus est, et sub ipso splendore, candidissimo pallio amictus est ab Angelis septem clarissimis, et juvenis apparuit juxta eum dans ei pacem, et dicens: Tu semper mecum eris.

24. Haec autem gerebantur intra domum Primiscrinii, nomine Nicostrati, apud quem custodiebantur Marcellianus et Marcus. Qui Nicostratus habebat uxorem, nomine Zoen: haec ante sex annos aegritudinis nimietate facta est muta, prudentiam tamen audiendi et intelligendi non solum non amiserat, verum etiam melius quam prius habuerat aurium officium obtinebat. Haec itaque cum intellexisset omnia, quae B. Sebastianus dixerat, et tantum lumen circa eum vidisset; cumque omnes tremefacti miraculi stupore tenerentur, innuebat manu omnibus, ut quasi exprobrandi essent, qui tam evidenti assertioni non crederent, et genibus ejus advoluta rogare eum manuum indiciis coepit. Sed S. Sebastianus cum videret eam cordis secreta linguae expressione declarare non posse, causas hujus silentii percunctatus, didicit sermonis illi copiam nimia vi infirmitatis ablatam. Tunc B. Sebastianus dixit: Si ego verus Christi servus sum, et si vera sunt omnia quae ex ore meo haec mulier audivit et credidit, jubeat Dominus meus Jesus Christus, ut redeat ad eam officinm linguae, et aperiat os ejus qui aperuit os Zachariae prophetae sui; et fecit crucem in os ejus. Atque ad hanc vocem S. Sebastiani, exclamavit mulier voce magna, dicens: Beatus es tu, et benedictus sermo oris tui: et beati qui credunt per te Christum Filium Dei vivi. Ego enim vidi oculis meis angelum ad te venientem de coelo, et librum ante oculos tuos tenentem, ex cujus lectione universa sermonis tui oratio decurrebat. Benedicti qui in omnibus quae locutus es credunt, et maledicti qui dubitaverint vel in uno verbo ex his omnibus quae

audierunt: quoniam sicut aurora superveniens universas tenebras noctis excludit et omnium oculis lumen, quod nox caeca negaverat reddit; ita lux sermonum tuorum omnem caliginem, omnemque ignorantiae caecitatem extersit, et oculis recte credentium serenum post noctis tenebras diem reddidit: a me autem non solum incredulitatis tenebras exclusit, verum etiam sermonis mei ostium, quod per sex annos clausum erat, patefecit.

25. Videns autem Nicostratus, vir ejus, quod esset tanta virtus Christi in sua uxore celebrata, coepit pedibus ejus advolvi, et indulgentiam petere, pro hoc quod imperiali et praefectorio jussu Sanctos Dei habuisset in vinculis: et auferens ex manibus eorum ferreos nexus genua eorum amplexus, coepit rogare ut dignarentur abscedere, dicens: O quam beatus essem si pro vestra mereri possem salute constringi! Forsitan sanguinis mei effusione abluerer, ut mortem illam poenarum aeternarum evaderem, et ad illam vitam pertingerem, quam nobis Deus per os domini mei Sebastiani manifestare dignatus est.

CAPUT VII. Marcelliani et Marci constantia, oratio ad neophytos.

26. Cumque rogaret Marcellianum et Marcum ut abscederent, dixerunt ei: Si tu fidei gloriam, quam numquam habueras accepisti; quomodo nos quam fidem semper ab infantia habuimus, relinquentes, tibi passionis nostrae calicem damus, quem nos tibi propinare possumus, non donare? Dives est enim in omnibus Christus, et larga ubertatis suae affluentia omnibus venientibus meliora exhibet quam rogatur. Si enim cum essetis increduli, donatum est vobis lumen veritatis agnoscere; quanto magis credentibus vobis omnia quaecumque jam poscitis donabuntur? Divina enim clementia semper parata est vobis omnibus gratis praestare: et eo unumquemque gratiae suae dono multiplicat, quo mens ejus altioris fidei susceperit normam. Fides igitur vestra a magisterio sumpsit exordium, et omnia quae eruditio annosa vix confert, spatio unius

horae cepistis. Nulla vos memoria parentum impedit credere. Nullus tenerae aetatis in filios et vestros revocat nutritus affectus. Contemnitis subito quod semper amastis, et quaeritis quod numquam scistis. Per ignaras ingressi vias subito pervenistis ad Christum, et animo jam intrastis coelum, quia in terra nullum solatium requisistis. O incomparabile facti praeconium! o quam imitabile virtutis exemplum! Nondum vos ad Christum sacri baptismatis unda perduxit, nondum per tirocinii initia militaria saltem signa sumpsistis; et jam pro vero Rege arma arripitis, et ejus milites a vinculo ferri solventes, vos ipsos intrepidos optatis pro occidendis occidi.

27. Cum haec audientes omnes pariter fletibus poenitentiam praeteritae persuasionis ostenderent, Marcus ait: Discite, parentes charissimi, et vester, o conjuges, discat jugalis affectus, adversus pugnam diaboli, et contra omnes sagittas affectuum carnalis desiderii clypeum virtutum opponere, atque inter acies tyrannici exercitus hosti non cedere, dimicare acrius, gradum tenere, et ad regem fortiter pervenire. Insurgant quantum volunt, et saeviant satellites daemonum, et quibus volunt poenis corpora dilanient nostra; corpus occidere possunt, sed animam vincere non possunt pro fidei pugnantem veritate. Gloriosiores faciunt milites vulnera pro Imperatore suscepta: in hoc enim diabolus tyrannidis suae furore nunc saevit, in quo praevidet perseverantiae vestrae tropaeo se posse torqueri: et ideo tormenta infert, ne spes ejus pereat: mortem minatur, ut terreat; vitam promittit ut eripiat; securitatem pollicetur, ut tollat. Haec tota belli calliditas, hoc fraudis consilium, a suppliciis eripere corpus et vitiis animam subjugare. Nos e contra contendamus hosti non cedere, corpus contemnere, animae subvenire. Cur enim fortissimi duces militibus miserrimis terga convertant, et in eo bello deficiant, in quo possunt esse victores? Vel qua ratione mori timeant, qui sciunt hanc hominis naturam esse, non poenam? Cur, inquam, mori timeant, qui credunt istam vitam, falsam esse, et veram vitam inveniri non posse, nisi qui ab animo suo falsam istam abjecerit,

et caducam, quae non aliud amatoribus suis, nisi peccata imperat, suadet facinora, ingerit criminosa; nihilque aliud a suis amatoribus exigit, nisi ut penitus de perenni vita non cogitent, et regnum Dei futurum esse desperent?

28. Nunc videamus quibus casibus subjacet, quibusque periculis servit ancilla, ut cum eam probaverimus nec seipsam posse regere, servitia nostra ab ejus dominatione tollentes, alteram cui merito serviendum sit, requiramus. Quantos enim amatores ejus ruina subito gravis oppressit, fragor coeli percussit, fulmen incendit, naufragia perdiderunt, texit chaos, Charybdis ebibit, gladius jugulavit! et istam miseri cum doloribus amittentes vitam, illam penitus invenire non possunt! Ad illam etenim vitam non ducit tortura, sed causa. Uno denique eodemque poenarum genere et innocentibus salus aeterna confertur, et poena delinquentibus irrogatur.

CAPUT IX. Caeteri a Sebastiano una cum captivis conversi.

29. Igitur cum haec et his similia Marcus prosequeretur, coeperunt omnes qui aderant Deo gratias agere, atque universi flentes poenitudinem gerebant, quod charitati Dei praetulerant amorem carnis; et quia ab agone martyrii ausi fuissent animos revocare sanctorum. Cumque omnes, qui ad decipiendos sanctos venerant, unanimiter crederent Christo, Nicostratus cum conjuge sua urgebat se dicens: Non cibum capiam, neque potum, nisi mysterium mihi christianae religionis fuerit traditum. Cui S. Sebastianus dixit: Muta dignitatem tuam, et esse magis incipe Christi primiscrinius, quam praefecti. Audi itaque consilium meum, et omnes quos carcer inclusit, quos vincula tenent, quos ergastula conficiunt, in unum redige. Quod cum feceris, antistitem sacrosanctae legis adhibebo, ut cum omnibus qui credere voluerint mysterii suscipias sacramentum. Si enim diabolus Christo sanctos suos auferre conatus est, et conatur; quanto magis nos pietatis argumento hos, quos diabolus injuste

lucratus est curare debemus, et suo restituere Creatori? Et Nicostratus ad haec respondit, dicens: Quomodo iniquis et criminosis possunt sancta committi? S. Sebastianus dixit: Salvator noster pro peccatoribus suam nobis exhibere dignatus est praesentiam et ostendit mysterium, per quod omnia peccata et crimina homini auferantur, et omnes virtutes Domini conferantur. Inter initia igitur conversionis tuae hoc munus primum si tu conferas Christo, praesto erit remunerationis ejus praemium super te, corona martyrii, habens secum virtutum omnium flores immarcescibiles, aeternae vitae gaudiis profuturos. Audiens haec Nicostratus primiscrinius, abiit ad Claudium Commentariensem, et jussit universas personas ad domum ejus adducere, dicens: Quoniam proxima sessione omnes discutiendi sunt, volo ut cum illis Christianis, qui apud me sunt, praesto sint, ne aliqua praefectoriae discussioni deesse possit persona.

30. Igitur cum omnes ad domum primiscrinii perducti starent, catenarum nexibus vincti, hoc modo eos vir Dei Sebastianus alloquitur: Crimina diabolica si divinis virtutibus cedant, reatus vester a morte excluditur, et a gaudiis fugitivis revocatur. Egerat enim per suos satellites hostis injustus, ut animos militum Christi ad virtutum culmen erectos everteret, et in ipso perfectionis fastigio positos, ad coenum conaretur mergere inferorum. Hac de causa incaluit animus hostium dimicatione provocatus, ut vos, quos jam lucratus fuerat inimicus, de ejus captivitate tollentes, vestro vos Creatori reddamus. Diabolus enim nec dominus vester, nec creator, nec pater esse dignoscitur: Deus autem et Pater et Dominus et Conditor comprobatur. Et si hunc derelinquentes ad illum abistis, qui in tantum vestri exstitit inimicus, ut vos ad poenas perpetuae mortis adduceret, et ad istum lethalem faceret exitum devenire; quanto magis ad eum redeundum est, qui unicum Filium suum passioni et morti tradidit, ut nos a passionibus aeternis, et a morte perpetua liberaret? Cum haec et his similia prosequeretur S. Sebastianus, prostraverunt se cum lacrymis universi, et flexis

genibus coeperunt cordis gemitum reddere, et se peccasse et impie egisse poenitentia vocibus exclamare. Fundebant ergo amaras lacrymas, et se velle Christo credere, unanimis vocibus resonabant. Tunc B. Sebastianus jubet eos omnes a vinculis catenarum exsolvi.

CAPUT X. Omnes a Polycarpo ad baptismum praeparati.

31. Post haec S. Sebastianus abiit ad Polycarpum presbyterum, ubi erat causa persecutionis occultus, et narravit ei omnia quae gesta sunt. Quibus auditis S. Polycarpus gratias egit Deo, et una cum eo venit ad domum Nicostrati primiscrinii, et videns turbas credentium, salutans eos cum omni gaudio dixit: Beati omnes vos, qui audistis vocem Domini nostri Jesu Christi dicentis: Venite ad me omnes qui laboratis et onerati estis, et ego vos requiescere faciam. Tollite jugum meum super vos, et discite a me quia mitis sum, et humilis corde; et invenietis requiem animabus vestris. Jugum enim meum suave est, et onus meum leve (Matth. XI, 28 seqq.). Vos itaque fratres nostri, quos nondum baptismatis unda diluit, et consecrando Deo omnipotenti charissimos filios fecit, pro hoc quod a proposito sancto revocare conati estis beatissimos milites Christi, opus vobis erat poenitentia, ut per ipsam ad indulgentiam veniretis. Nunc autem quia ad tantam gloriam accessistis, ut etiam ad passionem a qua dolenter alios revocare voluistis, ad ipsam desideretis gratanter velle currere et libenter amplecti, sciatis vos et ad indulgentiam pervenisse, et ad palmam attingere. Vetus hoc est artificium Christi. Nam ipsum quem vas electionis suae dignatus est et voluit magistrum gentibus dare, qui non solum fidelium animos a pietatis proposito revocabat, sed etiam nolentes a Christo discedere lapidibus obruebat; hunc nobis ipse Dominus apostolum condonavit, tribuitque nobis ex Saulo Paulum, ex apostata fecit apostolum, et dedit Ecclesiae suae ex persecutore doctorem. Amator passionis factus est is, qui persecutionis auctor exstiterat: et qui in alienis afflictionibus prius gratulabatur, in suis postmodum

persecutionibus laetabatur. Ipse ergo qui tunc in apostolo suo virtutem istam exercuit, ipse et nunc de ipso inferorum conclavi, et ex ipsis draconum faucibus animarum vestrarum captivitatem eripuit, et vobis nunc a tenebris ad lucem remeantibus aeternae vitae januas patefecit. Quia ergo omnes daemones, qui sunt tenebrarum filii, contristantur, unde et omnes sancti angeli, qui sunt filii lucis, gratulantur; accedat unusquisque vestrum, et det nomen suum, ut hodierno die usque ad vesperam percurrente jejunio, festivum baptismatis sacramentum opportunum tempus inveniat. Justum est enim, ut lux a mortali mundo abscedens ad nostras mentes immortales accedat, ut qui in isto saeculo volutati in luto tenebrarum sumus, aqua sanctificationis abluti ac mundati, et sinceritate induti alacres pergamus ad Christum. Haec et his similia prosequente S. Polycarpo universi gavisi sunt, et unusquisque nomen suum festinabat priusquam interrogaretur offerre.

CAPUT XI. Baptizati catechumeni, unaque Claudius cum filiis.

32. Cumque haec agerentur, venit Claudius commentariensis ad primiscrinii Nicostrati domum, ubi ista agebantur; et dicit Nicostrato. Vehementer praefectura commota est, quod personas reorum tuae domus custodiae tradi jussisti. Hac de causa suis te jussit praefectus aspectibus praesentari. Vide quasi debeas interrogatus dare responsum. Ingressus itaque ad praefectum Nicostratus cum interrogatus fuisset, cur eas personas, quas carceris claustra retinebant, suae voluerit domus mancipari custodiae, respondit: Amplitudinis vestrae jussu christianas intra domum meam custodiendas suscepi personas, quibus ut terrorem passionis incuterem, reorum illos feci sociari personis, ut jussioni vestrae et persuasioni nostrae si non consensu suo, saltem alieno experimento consentiant, et metuant ne similis eos poena concludat. Libentissime igitur haec audiens praefectus dimisit eum dicens: Magno te censu

a parentibus eorum remunerari faciam, cum per te illis fuerint incolumes filii restituti.

33. Revertens itaque ad domum suam Nicostratus primiscrinius cum Claudio commentariensi, coepit universa referre, et qualiter S. Sebastianus, cum sit amicus imperatorum, christianissimus sit, et in eruditione divina perfectus, et qualiter animas christianorum sua exhortatione revocasset, et quod satis idonea ratione docuisset istam vitam fugitivam et imaginariam esse, et sic dum teneri putatur, auferri. Narrabat etiam, quomodo veniens repente lux de coelo perlustrasset eum, et quomodo uxorem ejus, quae per sex annos muta fuerat, fecit loqui.

34. Cum haec narrasset Nicostratus Claudio, corruit ad pedes Nicostrati Claudius, dicens: Ex amissa conjuge duos filios habeo, ex quibus unus hydropis morbo fatigatur, alius diversis vulneribus opprimitur; rogo ut jubeas eos visitari. Non enim dubito quod ille, qui potuit facere ut post sex annos loqueretur uxor tua, faciat, si voluerit, ut ad filios meos sanitas redeat. Et haec dicens proripuit se ad domum suam, et fecit inter manus adduci duos filios suos, et introducens eos intra domum, ubi erant sancti Dei, projecit eos ante pedes eorum dicens: Nulla penitus dubietatis signa in corde meo remanserunt: sed ex toto corde credens quod Christus, quem colitis, ipse sit verus Deus, detuli huc vobis duo incrementa mea, credens quod possent per vos a mortis periculo liberari. Dicunt ei omnes simul sancti Dei: Omnes quos hic hodie infirmitas aliqua tenet, mox ut christiani facti fuerint, sanabuntur.

35. Cumque clamaret Claudius credere se, et desiderare fieri Christianum, jussit S. Polycarpus ut darent singuli nomina sua. Primus itaque omnium dedit nomen suum Tranquillinus pater Marcelliani et Marci. Post hunc sex amici eorum, id est, Ariston, Crescentianus, Eutychianus, Urbanus, Vitalis et Justus;

post hos Nicostratus primiscrinius, et Castorius frater ejus, et Claudius Commentariensis. Post hos filii Claudii, Felicissimus et Felix. Post hos Marcia mater Marcelliani et Marci cum uxoribus eorum et filiis: simul autem et Symphorosa uxor Claudii, et Zoe uxor Nicostrati. Post hos omnis familia quae erat in domo Nicostrati, animae triginta et tres promiscui sexus et aetatis, dehinc omnes qui vincti fuerant, ac de carceris squalore adducti, animae sedecim.

36. Igitur omnes isti LXVIII, a S. Polycarpo presbytero baptizati, et a S. Sebastiano suscepti sunt; feminarum autem matres factae sunt Beatrix et Lucina. Primum itaque Claudii filios, hydropicum unum et alterum vulneribus plenum, mox ubi in nomine sanctae Trinitatis intinxit; ita de fonte sani elevati sunt, ut nec signum in eis alicujus morbi praeteriti remansisset. Post hos autem infantulos Tranquillinus pater SS. Marcelliani et Marci, qui ita podagrico et chiragrico fuerat dolore constrictus, ut sicut supra dictum est, vix in manibus portaretur. Hunc dum exuerent indumentis, et ille intolerabili se diceret dolore torqueri, interrogat eum Polycarpus presbyter, dicens: Tranquilline, si ex toto corde credis unigenitum Filium Dei Dominum Jesum Christum tibi salutem posse conferre, et omnibus peccatis tuis indulgentiam condonare, proprio ore edicito. Tranquillinus respondit: Ego indulgentiam solam peccatis meis dari et desidero et credo. Caeterum, etsi post baptismatis hujus sanctificationem in doloribus fuero, non potero de fide Christi ulterius dubitare: probavi enim et ex toto corde credens, in mea mente consensi, quod Filius Dei sit Dominus Jesus Christus, qui potest et animabus et corporibus salutem tribuere, et a morte aeterna ad vitam perpetuam revocare. Haec cum dixisset voce magna, omnes sancti prae gaudio lacrymas effundebant, et rogabant Dominum ut fidei ejus fructus ostenderetur. Sanctus igitur Polycarpus confessor et presbyter mox ut eum chrismatis linivit unguento, interrogavit eum iterum, si crederet in Patrem et Filium et Spiritum sanctum; statim ut respondit. Credo, resolutae

sunt manus ejus quae erant nodosae, et genua simul et plantae pedum ejus ita sunt incolumes redditae, ut ac si puerulus renovatis pedibus suis in fontem descenderet clamans et dicens: Tu es Deus unus et verus, quem miser iste mundus ignorat.

37. Hoc itaque ordine suo baptizato, universi, prout competebat, baptizati sunt, et per dies decem qui supererant dilationi, quam meruerant, in Dei laudibus perdurantes ducebant dies et noctes in hymnis et canticis, et quasi fideles milites parabant animos suos ad dimicandum pro Christi nomine in martyrio bellaturi, ita ut et in mulieribus et infantulis amor ferveret martyrii, et invicem se ad confessionem sancti nominis contra diabolicas acies praepararent.

CAPUT XII. Errores Gentilium coram Chromatio Urbis praefecto confutati a Tranquillino.

38. Diebus igitur acceptae dilationis expletis, Agrestius Chromatius urbis Romae praefectus ad se Tranquillinum patrem Marcelliani et Marci venire jubet. Quem cum de suorum perquireret arbitrio filiorum, Tranquillinus respondit: Ad referendas beneficiis vestris gratias nullus mihi oris sufficit sermo. Nisi enim currentes sententias vestri frena moderaminis tenuissent, et ego filios amisissem, et me patrem filii non haberent. Congratulantur mihi omnes, quos tenet paternus affectus, et pungit charitatis stimulus; etiam vestra, credo, quod mihi congaudeat celsitudo, quando morituris vita collata, et anxiis laetitia reddita, sollicitis securitas restituta.

39. Tunc praefectus aestimans filios ejus suas velle idolis inclinare cervices, ait: Venienti ergo die debita numinibus a filiis tuis thura reddantur: per quae et tu filiis perseveres incolumis, et tibi filii condonentur. Audiens haec Tranquillinus dixit: Illustrissime virorum, examinis vestri libram si velitis erga me et filios

meos aequa lance pensare, agnoscere poteritis hoc Christianum vocabulum magnae esse virtutis. Praefectus dixit: Insanis, Tranquilline. Tranquillinus respondit: Insaniam passus sum, et animae et corporis; sed statim ut credidi Christo, et animae meae recepi et corporis sanitatem.

40. Praefectus dixit: Ego, ut video, ad hoc inducias sceleratis filiis tuis dedisse cognoscor, ut non solum tu illos ab errore non tolleres, sed illi te suis erroribus irretirent. Tranquillinus dixit: Per gloriam vestram, nomen ipsum erroris discutite, et videte quae opera erroris nomine nuncupentur. Praefectus dixit: Tu dic quae opera erroris nomen accipiant. Tranquillinus dixit: Primus error est viam vitae relinquere, et per viam mortis gratanter incedere. Praefectus dixit: Et quae est via mortis? Tranquillinus dixit: Non tibi videtur via mortis esse, mortuis hominibus Deitatis nomen imponere, et figuras eorum per ligna et lapides adorare?

41. Praefectus dixit: Ergo non sunt dii quos colimus? Tranquillinus dixit: Intantum non sunt dii ut legatur in codicibus publicis, et quam male sint nati, et quam iniquos et crudeles et sceleratos parentes habuerint; et quam inique et dolose et fraudulenter vixerint; et quam miserabiliter mortui sint. Numquid antequam Saturnus Cretensibus imperaret, et filiorum suorum carnes comederet, Deus in coelis non erat, aut Creta insula habebat regem, et coeli Deum non habebant? Valde errat qui putat Jovem filium ejus, imperare fulminibus, homuncionem in quo malitia et libido regnabat. Quem non persecutus est, qui patri non pepercit? Aut quam sordem non exercuit, qui suam germanam accepit uxorem? In foro, in plateis, in domibus, atque in omni loco quotidie legimus, quia sordidissima Juno quod et soror et conjux fuerit gloriatur: et rapti Ganymedis honor turpissimus atque incestissimus ab ipsis, a quibus Jovis colitur, non negatur. Non ergo erras, vir sublimissime, qui tales colis, quales Romanae jubent leges pro sui facti qualitate damnari, et relicto

Deo omnipotente qui in coelis regnat, lapidi dicis, Deus meus es tu: et ligno dicis: Adjuva me?

42. Praefectus dixit: Ex quo coepistis blasphemare deos, et a cultura eorum recedere, ex eo diversis cladibus Romanus orbis opprimitur. Tranquillinus respondit: Non est verum. Nam si recenseas decadas stylo Livii digestas, illic invenies Jovi thura ponentes, una die viginti tria millia Romani exercitus juvenes cecidisse. Sed et illud non es immemor, quod Senonenses Galli etiam Capitolium occupaverunt et omnem Romanam manum suis ludibriis subjugarunt. Diversas fames, et inenarrabiles pestes, diversas captivitates, diversas effusiones sanguinis Romanus orbis passus est, antequam unum colerent homines Deum. Nunc vero ex quo invisibilis et verus Deus coepit a credentibus coli, aucta pace exsultat Romanum imperium. Sed quod pejus est, Deus, qui hoc praestat, non cognoscitur; sed creaturae ejus ascribitur, quidquid a Creatore praestatur.

43. Praefectus dixit: Si ille colendus est, qui humanis commodis aliquid praestat, nullus nisi sol habebitur deus, qui aspectu suo terrae viscera vegetat, ut semina suscepta parturiat, et genuinae sobolis grana in culmo restituat, atque universis salutis nostrae utilitatibus, et lumen et restaurationem pariter tribuat et vigorem. Tranquillinus respondit: Et in hoc error est infinitus. Nam si hodie per servum suum quispiam clientibus suis tribuat quod rogatur, infinita stultitia est, si neglectus ille qui praestitit, servus per quem praestiterit honoretur. Et ut aliquam hujus dicti comparationem exhibeam; numquid cum naves Romanis alimenta deferunt, navibus potiusquam regibus gratiae referuntur? Si ergo non navigantibus, sed imperantibus, homines quod annonantur ascribunt, quanto magis soli Deo agendae sunt gratiae, cujus nutu et haec omnibus usibus nostris elementa deserviunt, et sol ipse quotidie terrae marique pariter et clauditur in fine diei, et in diei iterum renovatione aperitur?

CAPUT XIII. Verbi incarnatio Gentili exposita.

44. Praefectus dixit: Si ergo unus et invisibilis est quem colitis, Christum, quem Judaei crucifixerunt, non colitis? Tranquillinus dixit: recte haec inquireres, si credere destinares. Incredulis enim omne quod nolunt vanum videtur. Semel enim in praeceps voluntas mortalium declinans, omne quod vituperat vituperari desiderat; et vult ut laudetur ab omnibus omne quod laudat. Sed sapiens pro merito suo cuicumque rei, aut vituperationem suam impendere nititur aut laudem. Praefectus dixit: Ego te de Christo vestro interrogo. Si enim a vobis hoc colitur quod istis oculis non videtur, Christum non colitis qui et visus est, et auditus, et interrogatus, et omnia quae humanae fragilitati competunt in ejus leguntur passione completa? Tranquillinus dixit: Audi similitudinem et intellige veritatem: Verbi gratia, si hodie annulum tuum habentem gemmam pretiosam videas in cloaca, aut in sterquilinio volutantem, et ad hunc eruendum mittas servos tuos; illi autem nec illum potuerint liberare, sed et seipsos in aliquo dum illum conantur eripere, polluerint; postea vero tu ipse, deponens has sericas quas indutus es vestes, induas te servilem tunicam et descendens in cloacam mittas manus tuas in stercoribus, et annulum aureum simul tuis manibus repraesentes et gemmam, prae gaudio omnes amicos tuos invitas ad epulas et laetaris super annulum et gemmam, quod sint de nimiis squaloribus liberata. Praefectus dixit: Hanc propositionem ad cujus similitudinem attulisti? Tranquillinus respondit: Ut ostenderem tibi unum invisibilem Deum nos colere. Praefectus dixit: Et quod est aurum? aut quae est gemma, quae in sterquilinio volutabatur? Tranquillinus respondit: Aurum, corpus humanum est, gemma vero anima est, quae in ipso corpore inclusa est. Corpus vero et anima unum hominem faciunt, quomodo aurum et gemma unum annulum facere comprobantur. Sed quantumvis pretiosus tibi sit annulus, longe satis homo pretiosior est centuplum et charus Christo. Tu misisti servos tuos, ut annulum de sordibus eriperent, et nulla ratione eum

eruere potuerunt. Misit et prophetas suos Deus de coelo loquens ad eos, ut humanum genus a sordibus hujus mundi eriperet: et nulla ratione omnino hoc facere vel instantia potuerunt. Tu deposuisti aureas vestes, et servili indumento indutus descendisti in cloacam, et manus tuas misisti in sordibus, ut annulum de sordibus liberares: Exuit et se majestas Divinitatis suae splendore, non tamen superna relinquens; et induit se servili nostri corporis indumento, et huc in cloacam hujus mundi coelo descendens, misit manus suas in sordibus passionum nostrarum; et passionem, quae meritis nostris debebatur, in semetipso suscipiens, gloriae nos suorum reddidit digitorum. Nam qui per incredulitatem volutabamur in squaloribus mundi, per fidem abluti a sordibus, divinis sumus manibus, ut ille tuus annulus, restituti. Numquid servi tui, qui te negaverunt dominum suum, dum te in habitu servili respicerent, non potuerunt ut rebelles occidi? Ita et qui negant Christum Dominum suum pro hoc quod semetipsum a majestate exinanivit, et formam servi suscepit, nullatenus poterunt aeterni ignis poenas evadere. Ideo denique nobis qui in eum credimus, aeterni fontis unda subvenit, ut aeternus ignis ab aeterno fonte vincatur, et infidelitas a fidelitate superetur.

45. Praefectus dixit: Ut video, non ut filios tuos ab hac intentione tolleres poposcisse probaris inducias, sed ut has aniles fabulas ad nostra tribunalia meditatus afferres. Tranquillinus dixit: Non meditantur discipuli Christi quid in conspectu judicum prosequantur. Sic enim praemonuit dicens: Quando potestatibus hujus mundi vos causa mei nominis tradent, nolite cogitare quomodo aut quid loquamini, dabitur enim vobis divinitus in illa hora quid loquamini. Non enim vos estis qui loquimini, sed Spiritus Dei, qui loquitur in vobis (Matth. X, 19). Non ergo meditando ego, sed credendo inveni Creatorem meum, et qui eram podagrico et chiragrico dolore contractus et quassatus, statim ut Christo credidi, ac si parvulus omnium membrorum meorum recepi sanitatem. Constat ergo apud animum meum, ipsum me creasse qui me

renovare dignatus est, et sicut dedit restaurationem corpori, ita quoque animae post istam vitam dare promisit, si tamen non dubius nec timidus hominum terroribus frangar; sed in ejus nominis confessione perdurans fidem integram, quam me Deus fecit invenire, conservem.

46. Praefectus dixit: Ignoras, Tranquilline, quanta invictissimorum principum erga Christianos ira desaeviat, et ideo quasi securus quod tibi videtur sine timore prosequeris. Tranquillinus dixit: Stultus timor est, quo plus timetur humana indignatio, quam divina. Numquid si in medio canum latrantium venerimus, et vano furore nos coeperint suis morsibus attrectare, possunt nobis de animo tollere hoc quod nos homines sumus rationabiles, cum sint illi canes, et irrationabiles, et insani? Ita qui nobis recte credentibus irascuntur, saevire quidem possunt, et inferre iniqua supplicia; numquam tamen de corde nostro hoc auferre poterunt, quod Dominum Jesum Christum et creatorem esse credimus, et redemptorem nostrum ac restauratorem esse gaudemus. Tum praefectus jussit eum recipi a Commentariis, dicens: Proxima te audiam sessione.

CAPUT XIV. Chromatius Urbis praefectus catechizatur.

47. Post haec mittit et adduci eum ad se praecepit per noctem occulte, et offerens ei infinitum pondus auri dicebat: Ostende mihi medicamentum ex quo recuperasti salutem. Cui Tranquillinus ait: Scias grandem iram et furorem Dei passuros esse, qui gratiam ejus vel venundandam existimant vel emendam. Unde si vis a podagrico dolore liberari, crede Christum Filium Dei, et liberaberis, et sicut hodie me vides, ita salvus eris. Nempe vix manibus deferebar, et undecim annos per omnes juncturas nervorum in corpore meo dolorum nodis astrictus, vix ori meo panis alienis manibus tradebatur: illico ut

Christum verum Deum esse credidi, salutis meae gaudia recepi, et sum incolumis, quia verum Deum salvatorem meum agnovi.

48. Tunc praefectus dimisit eum dicens: Adduc ad me qui te Christianum fecit, ut si mihi promiserit sanitatem, possim et ego fieri Christianus. Statim autem Tranquillinus veniens ad S. Polycarpum presbyterum narravit ei omnia quae gesta vel dicta sunt; et ducens eum intra domum occulte, praefecti eum aspectibus praesentavit. Cui praefectus ait: Licet gravis animadversio principum Christianis infesta sit, tamen spe recuperandae salutis afferam vobis quidquid illud est usque ad dimidium bonorum patrimonii mei, si ab hac nodositate condylomatum mei fuerint membra corporis resoluta. Tunc S. Polycarpus subridens ait: Potens est Dominus Jesus Christus ut ignorantiae tuae januas aperiat, et ostendat tibi quod ipse sit corporis tui restaurator. Nam pecuniam sive qui afferunt, sive qui oblatam accipiunt, non solum nullam dolentibus conferunt medicinam, sed etiam ipsi sibi insanabilem morbum assumunt. Dicit ei praefectus: Dic ergo mihi quid faciam, ut consequi valeam quod spero. Dicit ei Polycarpus: Si credideris ex toto corde tuo, sicut credidit Tranquillinus, salvus eris. Dicit ei praefectus: Quo ordine credere debeam intimato? Tunc S. Polycarpus catechizavit eum, et indixit ei ut per triduum jejunaret. Et convocans ad se S. Sebastianum tribus diebus et tribus noctibus jejunavit cum eo: et cum lacrymis pariter orabant, ut fidem nominis sui in salutem volentis credere Dominus declararet.

CAPUT XV. Chromatii confracta Idola.

49. Igitur cum dies tertia, quae constituta fuerat, advenisset, ad domum sustinentis praefecti veniunt pariter properantes. Qui ingressi dixerunt: Pax fidei tuae. At ille resalutavit eos officiosissime; et hortatur eos sedere juxta se, et dixit: Ex ore Tranquillini ratio egressa oculorum meorum assertione declaratur.

Video enim hunc sanissimum quem podagrico et chiragrico videram dolore contractum. A quo genus medicamenti unde fuisset salvatus inquirens, tale ab eo recepi responsum: Dum fidem meam in idolis ponerem, debilis et nimia sum infirmitate contractus: at ubi unum Deum in coelis didici ostensione Christianorum, abnegavi universa quae sine causa colueram, et tradidi fidem animi mei Christo. Mox autem ut unum et verum Deum in coelis regnare confessus sum, statim omnis, quam per undecim annos amiseram, ad me reversa est sanitas, et omnis a me est protinus infirmitas separata. Haec audivi auribus, probavi oculis, corde credidi; superest ut quod fecistis Tranquillino et mihi faciatis, ut possim mei corporis recipere sanitatem.

50. Polycarpus presbyter dixit: Si transeuntes dolores anima hominis non suffert, quid de illis doloribus actura est, quibus nullus umquam evenit finis, nulla datur omnino successio? Nam isti dolores illorum dolorum imaginem portant, et quantum distat inter ignem vivum et picturam ejus, tantum distat inter dolores quos nunc patitur corpus, et illos quos anima passura est, si ignara Creatoris sui praesentis vitae impleverit munus. Age ergo nobiscum prius de doloribus illis, et esto de illa poena sollicitus, quae habet ignem semper ardentem, et vermem semper edentem.

51. Tunc Chromatius urbis Romae praefectus, cum unico filio suo Tiburtio, dedit nomen suum dicens: In hoc de fide mea certos vos esse convenit, in qua etiam filium meum Christianum fieri mecum exopto. S. Sebastianus dixit: Vide ne sola recuperatione tui corporis ductus te Christianum fieri speres, sed magis spe vitae aeternae facias mentem tuam puram ad videndam rationem veritatis. Nisi enim agnoveris qui sit Creator tuus, non poteris invenire salutem quam quaeris. Chromatius dixit: Ergo et rusticos et simplicissimos homines non videmus esse Christianos, ita ut inter mille viros vix invenias unum qui possit vel sermonum disciplinam adipisci. Numquid hi omnes ad istam inquisitionem

attingere potuerunt dum fierent Christiani? S. Sebastianus ait: Hoc responsum tuum nostrae partis firmat assertionem. Nam ab origine mundi cum ruricolis et pastoribus ovium Deus habuit rationem, et juxta finem mundi veniens non elegit grammaticos et oratores, sed piscatores et simplices, et ipsis tradidit notitiam suam.

52. Chromatius dixit: Cur ergo me dicis prius debere agnoscere quis sit creator meus, quem nisi agnoverim salutem invenire non possim? S. Sebastianus dixit: Quia multos deos, et multas deas coluisti. Nisi ergo hos a corde tuo excluseris, et imagines eorum confregeris, et cognoveris unum et verum Deum, vitam et salutem invenire non poteris. Chromatius dixit: Indica ergo mihi quis sit unus et verus Deus. S. Sebastianus respondit: Si servum tuum ad hauriendam aquam miseris, dum ad fontem venerit, aspicit prius ne sordes aliquae intus lateant in lagena, et non est ausus aquam in vas mittere, nisi mundatum a sordibus viderit; nos tibi quomodo poterimus tradere fontem veritatis, nisi prius te ab omnibus idolorum sordibus et squaloribus feceris alienum? Chromatius dixit: Et quo ordine alienus effici potero ab his? S. Sebastianus dixit: Da nobis potestatem ut omnia idola, quae in domo tua invenerimus, lapidea confringamus, lignea incendamus, aurea et argentea vel aerea conflemus, et pretia eorum egentibus dividamus. Chromatius dixit: Et cum haec feceritis, mihi quid fructus accedet? S. Sebastianus dixit: Omnium nervorum tuorum, quorum nodositate constringeris, statim consequeris sanitatem; et quasi qui numquam dolueris, ita pedibus tuis currere incipies, et agnoscere quod inimicos tuae salutis deos dilexeris; tuum vero parentem hunc esse, qui te statim ut ejus notitiam atque culturam inveneris, restaurat et salvat.

53. Chromatius dixit: Nolite vosmetipsos ad hanc injuriam deponere: sed servis meis praecipiam; et ipsi universa confringent. S. Sebastianus dixit: Dubii et timidi et infideles si ea confregerint, inveniet diabolus per quamcumque

negligentiam eorum occasionem laedendi eos, et statim ut laesi fuerint, dicent infideles, propterea eos laesos esse quia idola confregerunt. Nisi enim loricam habens non eripitur ictibus sagittarum. Galea enim et scuto et hasta utitur docta manus in praelio, ut ex munimine armorum et impetu feriendi assumat audaciam, et terga non vertat. Similiter et milites Dei, qui scuto fidei muniuntur, et lorica tegminis Christi proteguntur, habentes galeam fidei et salutis, ipsis est tutum inire certamen. Pugnant enim acerrime et fortiter vincunt, quia contra invisibilem hostem die noctuque infatigabiliter praeliantur; et sunt tecti in omnibus membris, fide potius armati quam ferro. Chromatius dixit: Fiat volontas Dei et vestra. Tunc S. Polycarpus presbyter, et B. Sebastianus praecingentes se oraverunt; et post orationem amplius quam ducenta idolorum signa confringentes, coeperunt gratias agere Deo suo.

CAPUT XVI. Instvumentis astrologiae judiciariae confractis sanatur Chromatius.

54. Post haec accesserunt ad Chromatium dicentes ei: Confringentibus nobis idola tu debuisti sanitatem recipere, nisi forte aliqua tibi in animo signa infidelitatis derelinquuntur. Hoc enim apud nos certum gerimus, quod aut est aliquid, quod nondum est fractum; aut si omnia fracta sunt, quid in animo geras nobis evidentius manifesta. Tunc ille: Habeo, inquit, cubiculum holovitreum, in quo omnis disciplina stellarum ac mathesis mechanica est arte constructa, in cujus fabrica pater meus Tarquinius amplius quam ducenta pondo auri dignoscitur expendisse. Cui S. Sebastianus dixit: Si hoc tu integrum habere volueris, te ipsum frangis. Chromatius dixit: Quid enim? Mathesis aut ephemeris aliquo sacrificiorum usu coluntur, cum tantum eis mensium et annorum cursus certo numero per horarum spatia distinguuntur? et lunaris globi plenitudo vel diminutio, digitorum motu, rationis magisterio, et calculi computatione praevidetur? S. Polycarpus presbyter dixit: Illic signa Leonis et

Capricornii et Sagittarii, et Scorpionis, et Tauri sunt, illic in Ariete luna, in Cancro hora; in Jove stella, in Mercurio tropica, in Venere Mars, et in omnibus istis monstruosis daemonibus ars Deo inimica cognoscitur. Ista Christiani ita recusant, ut non solum ipsi non habeant, non colant, non credant, non teneant; verum etiam nec animos illos habeant, qui hujuscemodi nugis suum occupant pectus? Omnia enim ista falsa deceptionisque ministra sunt: similitudo in eis veritatis est, non ipsa veritas.

55. Dicit ei Chromatius: Quid? quod nonnumquam futura praenuntiant? S. Sebastianus dixit: Ista omnia vanissima esse et falsissima, Christo revelante, cognovimus; quae tibi nunc manifestius aperiemus. Praecipe hodie ad te mathesis venire doctorem, cui dicas, illo tempore te asperis casibus laborasse, et inquire per quas stellas hoc tibi evenerit mali; responsa ejus erunt procul dubio talia, quod tempus tuum a malitioso Marte susceptum est, aut Saturnus apocatasticus fuit, aut annus tuus ex diametro susceptus est, aut climacterica tibi in centro sunt nata, aut syndetus fuit cum malo, aut invisibilis, aut in schemate, aut immobilis circa te exstitit cursus in stellis. Haec et his similia cum dixerit, rationis tibi verisimile assignare nititur aliquid et probare. Age nunc, interroga alterum mathematicum, cui ipsas horas ipsumque tempus in bonis tibi exuberasse casibus dicas, illico videbis eum tibi rationabilia schemata infinita afferre, quibus approbet, quia in ipsis tibi temporibus evenire debuerint bona. Circulum etenim tenet ex omni parte collectum, in quo diversas et varias causas accipit, et quibus occasionem capiat dicendi quod voluerit.

56. Nam futura dum penitus praevidere non possunt, climactericas dicunt, id est naturae rei incerta profugia. Nam diversis temporibus nati uno naufragio perierunt, et una hora diei vel noctis exorti, alter ad mendicitatem deponitur, ascendit alter ad regnum: et in uno praelio innumerabilis multitudo

prosternitur, et uno die, imo uno puncto, in una domo, duae feminae, pudicissima altera, altera efficitur impudica: utriusque stellae si meritum contulerint, nec meretrix vituperanda est, nec casta laudanda. Certe legum latores et principes sacra sua praevaricata puniunt, et ideo forum, ideo judex, ideo jura, ut justi laudentur recte, et injusti merito puniantur. Et hoc nolo ut otiosum existimes, quod te ipsum nondum salvatum attendis. Nam si ex integro a te inimici generis humani caeremonias abjiceres, in temetipso quod verum est didicisses.

57. Audiens haec Chromatius dixit: Verus ille Deus est, qui vos tales probatur habere cultores. Nam omnis sermo vester ita rationibus affluit; ut et pecudum ad rationem veram mentes inclinet. Unde etiam hoc ipsum quod ad ornatum domus visus sum excepisse, ne impediat saluti meae ejus incolumitas, dissipetur. Credo enim, et haec fides mea est, quod his omnibus quae Christianitatis lex abominatur et prohibet, si a me ex integro separavero, et praesentem merear salutem consequi et futuram.

58. Audiens haec filius ejus Tiburtius dixit: Nulla patiar ratione hoc opus pretiosum et praecipuum et incomparabile dejici. Sed ne paternae saluti videar venire contrarius, deferantur duo clibani et accensi ante januam cubiculi praeparentur, ut dum destructum ab eis fuerit, et pater meus non receperit sanitatem, ambo in singulis clibanis ardentibus demergantur. Audiens haec pater ejus, prohibebat fieri. Sancti vero non solum non metuebant promissum exitium, verum etiam constanter praeparari clibanos hortabantur.

59. Tunc accesserunt ad universa idola crystallina et holovitrea, et omne opus illud mechanicum: et subito, dum sanctorum manibus frangerentur, apparuit ante oculos Chromatii juvenis, cujus facies flammeo radiabat aspectu et dixit ei: Misit me Dominus meus Jesus Christus, cui credidisti, ut omnium

membrorum tuorum recipias sanitatem. Ad hanc vocem sanissimus redditus coepit currere post juvenem, ut pedes ejus oscularetur. At ille dixit ei: Vide ne contingas me, quia nondum baptismatis sanctificatio te a squaloribus abluit idolorum. Videns haec Tiburtius filius ejus, advolvitur ad pedes S. Polycarpi. Ipse autem Chromatius praefectus astringebat plantas S. Sebastiani, et ambo una voce clamabant: Verus Deus est Christus, verus et omnipotens unigenitus Filius Dei, quem praedicatis boni ministri ejus.

CAPUT XVII. Chromatii et Tiburtii baptismus.

60. Tunc B. Sebastianus dixit Chromatio: Sicut ipse nosti, principatum primae cohortis ago, sed utrum sit militia hominis, nescire olim decrevi, nec vellem. Ad hoc tantum sub chlamyde latere volui, ut nutantium animos instruerem, et dubitantes constantes efficerem, ne passionum doloribus cederent, quos fides fecerat bellatores. Tu autem amplissimae potestatis apicem gerens, non potes temetipsum nec a spectaculis tollere, neque judicandis negotiis absentare. Simulans igitur aegritudinem, tibi ipsi postula successorem, ut possis liber ab occupationibus mundi, futurae vitae rudimenta suscipere, ut secunda nativitate iterum natus aeternis efficiaris parentibus proles. Eodem itaque die mittit ad amicos suos in palatio positos, per quos testimonialia scripta suscipiens, tirocinium divinae militiae antequam baptizaretur accepit.

61. Quid memorem, quam plenissimae fidei fuerit, quamque acris ingenii contra infidelium asserta constiterit? Sequens lectio manifestat. Nam in initio qualiter sit sacrosancti fontis unda perfusus, mentis ejus fides evidenter enituit. Interrogatus si crederet, dixit: Credo. Iterum interrogatus, utrum abrenuntiaret omnibus idolis, respondit: Abrenuntio. Prosecuta est interrogatio sacerdotis, utrum renuntiaret omnibus peccatis; at ille ait: Ista prius debuisti inquirere antequam has aulas regis coelorum intrarem. Nunc autem reinduam me non

baptizatus, ut omnibus prius, quibus sum iratus, indulgeam; omnibus debitoribus meis chirographa restituam; si cui aliquid violenter abstuli, integrum reddi praecipiam: duae mihi post uxoris obitum concubinae sunt, et istis dotem et maritis tradam, ab omni nexu servili, ingenuo, privato, vel publico actuum meorum exsolvam: et ita demum promittam renuntiaturum me omnibus peccatis diabolicis et voluptatibus mundi. Dicit ei Polycarpus presbyter: Beatiorem te coelestis unda perfundet, cum ea quae arbitrio tuo dicis te esse facturum, tota festinatione compleveris: nam et quadragesimae tempus ideo baptizandis injungitur, ut tot diebus ipsi discant renuntiaturos se esse omnibus artibus inimici et mundi commerciis, si qui verissime effici volunt Christiani.

62. Tunc Tiburtius juvenis sapientissimus dixit: Pater, si tibi pro renuntiandis negotiis tempus flagitas, ego qui adhuc suscepturus eram negotia fori, soli susceptionis voluntati renuntio: et qui futurus eram advocatus ad agendas causas mortalium, suscipiam Christianitatem, ad agendas actiones angelicas, cum unus esse coepero ex eorum numero, qui aeternam vitam accipiunt, et efficiuntur causidici sanctitatis. Tunc amplexatus est eum B. Sebastianus: quem cum baptizasset S. Polycarpus, ipse pater susceptionis ejus est factus.
63. Igitur dum pauci admodum transacti fuissent dies, omnibus rite abrenuntiatis a Chromatio mundi negotiis, suscepit Chromatius sacri baptismatis novitatem; et cum eodem ex familia ejus promiscui sexus mille quadringentae animae, quos omnes prius manumissionis gratia a servitutis nodo exsolvit, et donis optimis instruxit, dicens hoc: Illi qui Deum incipiunt habere patrem, servi hominis non debent esse.

CAPUT XVIII. Chromatius, praefectura Urbis abdicata, persecutionis tempore Christianos alit.

64. Erat autem papa urbis Romae nomine Caius, vir magnae prudentiae, magnaeque virtutis, imperantibus Carino, Diocletiano et Maximiano. Sed Diocletianus in Urbe erat cum Maximiano: Carinus autem erat cum omni exercitu in partibus Galliarum positus: et ejus intuitu lenta persecutio Diocletiani circa Christianos esse coeperat; quia Carinus habebat aliquos amicos, quos hujus tituli professio decorabat.

65. Igitur occiso Carino in civitate Maguntiaco Maximiano et Aquilino consulibus, facta est persecutio talis, ut nullus emeret vel venundaret aliquid nisi qui statunculis positis in eo loco, ubi emendi gratia ventum fuisset, thuris exhibuisset incensum. Circa insulas, circa vicos, circa nymphea quoque erant positi compulsores, qui neque emendi copiam darent, aut hauriendi aquam ipsam facultatem tribuerent, nisi qui idolis delibassent.

66. Tunc S. Caii episcopi consilio habito, Chromatius illustris vir omnes Christianos in domo sua suscepit, et universos ita fovebat, ut nullus omnino sacrificandi necessitati succumberet. Verum quia tanta vis persecutionis exstiterat, ut opinio ipsa Christianitatis ejus celari non posset, meruit ex sacro rescripto Chromatius ut medendi gratia in Campano littore moraretur, in quo erat lati cespitis dominus, tribuitque copiam omni Christiano ire volenti cum eodem ad persecutoris rabiem declinandam. Tunc orta est contentio inter S. Polycarpum, et B. Sebastianum; quis horum duorum in Urbe remaneret, et quis iret cum Chromatio, qui tantum populum susceperat Christianum. Quibus altercantibus venerabilis papa Caius dixit: Dum ambo passionis coronam quaeritis, acquisitum Domino populum desolatis. Unde mihi videtur, ut tu, frater Polycarpe, quia et sacerdotii rectum tramitem tenes, et scientia Dei

repletus es, pergas simul ad confortandas credentium mentes et animos dubios aedificandos. At ille his auditis quievit et blandum papae imperium aequanimiter tulit. Venit itaque dies Dominica, in qua Caius episcopus agens quae Dei sunt intra domum Chromatii, hac omnes alloquitur voce: Dominus noster Jesus Christus praescius fragilitatis humanae duos in se credentibus constituit gradus, confessionis scilicet et martyrii, ut hi qui martyrii pondus se posse perferre desperant, confessionis gratiam teneant, et dantes latus bellantibus, Christi militum, qui pro ejus sunt nomine pugnaturi, sollicitudinem gerant. Pergant itaque qui volunt una cum filiis nostris Chromatio et Tiburtio, et mecum in hac urbe qui voluerint maneant. Non enim nos terrarum spatia divident, quos Christi charitas nectit, nec absentiam vestram sentiunt oculi nostri, quia de interioris hominis vos intuemur aspectu.

67. Haec et his similia dicente papa Caio, exclamavit Tiburtius, vir clarissimus dicens: Obsecro te, pater et episcoporum episcope, ne me patiaris terga persequentibus dare. Mihi enim valde jucundum est et optabile, si possem millies pro vero Deo occidi, tantum ut illius vitae dignitatem inveniam, quam nullus mihi successor eripiat, cui nulla tempora finem imponant. Tunc S. Caius, congaudens fidei ejus lacrymas effundebat, orans ut omnes qui remanserant certamine victores existerent, triumphum martyrii capientes.

CAPUT XIX. SS. Sebastiani, Tiburtii, et aliorum praeclara facta in Urbe.

68. Remanserant autem cum venerabili Caio papa hi, Marcellianus et Marcus, simul quoque et pater eorum vir clarissimus Tranquillinus, item B. Sebastianus, et pulcherrimus juvenis, sed et mente pulchrior, S. Tiburtius, et Nicostratus ex primiscrinio cum fratre suo Castorio, et cum conjuge sua, Zoe nomine; item Claudius cum Victorino fratre suo et cum filio suo Symphoriano qui fuerat a morbo hydropis liberatus. Hi tantum, universis cum Chromatio

proficiscentibus, cum Caio episcopo remanserunt: Marcum et Marcellianum diaconii honore sanctificavit, Tranquillinum vero patrem eorum, fecit presbyterum. S. Sebastianum autem, qui ad multorum profectum sub specie militiae latebat, defensorem Ecclesiae instituit, caeteros vero subdiaconos fecit.

69. Sed quia tutus nullus inveniro poterat locus ad latebram confovendam, morabantur omnes apud Castulum quemdam Christianum zetarium palatii: qui Castulus ibidem in palatio, in superiori loco et valde altissimo commanebat. Ideo autem haec apta mansio probabatur, quia et ipse Castulus cum suis omnibus christianissimus erat; et lex data de sacrificiis cum ubique sui fervore desaeviret, in illis qui palatio adhaerebant, quia nec suspicio de eis esse poterat, celabatur. Erant ergo, ut diximus, omnes hi morantes cum sancto papa Caio apud Castulum zetarium, in ipsis superioribus palatii, et die noctuque gemitibus ac fletibus, et jejuniis atque orationibus occupati, exorabant Dominum, ut digni haberentur tolerantia confessionis ejus, in numero sanctorum martyrum sociari.

70. Ascendebant autem ad eos occulte religiosi viri et religiosae feminae, et a Sanctis diversas sibi sanitatum gratias impetrabant. Corroboratos namque verae fidei firmitate et solidato fundamento virtutum, sanitatum gratia prosequebatur. Nam et caecorum oculi illuminabantur eorum precibus, et sanabantur infirmi, et ex obsessis corporibus daemones pellebantur.

71. Interea dum haec aguntur, transiens B. Tiburtius occurrit homini qui de alto lapsus, et caput et omnia membra quassaverat, ita ut de sola sepultura ejus agerent hi, quorum filius esse dignoscebatur. Tunc dicit eis flentibus: Permittite me praecantare ei, forsitan recuperabit sanitatem. Cumque omnes dedissent spatium, accessit juxta eum, et dicens supra vulnera ejus lente

orationem Dominicam et symbolum, ita solidata sunt ossa ejus, et caput et omnia viscera, ut quasi nihil ei evenisset, ita factus sit incolumis.

72. Haec itaque cum fecisset coepit ire. Tenebant autem illum parentes ejus dicentes: Veni et habe eum servum et omnia bona nostra tibi tradimus cum eo, quia ipsum unicum, quem habebamus, nobis jam mortuum reddi listi vivum. Dicit eis: Si ea quae vobis dixero feceritis, magni pendam mercedem sanitatis hujus. Dicunt ei parentes ejus: Nosmetipsos si servos habere digneris, contraire non possumus: quin immo et optamus, si ipse judicaveris dignum. Tunc apprehendens manus eorum, segregavit eos a turbis, et indicavit eis virtutem nominis Christi. Et videns animum eorum fixum fortiter in timore Domini, perduxit eos ad papam Caium et dixit: Venerabilis papa ac divinae legis antistes, ecce quos per me hodie lucratus est Christus, in quibus fides mea velat arbuscula novella, primum prorupit in fructum. Tunc S. Caius episcopus baptizavit eos, hoc est, juvenem cum parentibus suis, Deo gratias referentes.

CAPUT XX. SS. Zoes. Tranquillini et aliorum coedes.

73. Verum quia multum est si velimus ea prosequi quae et quanta per eos fecerit Christus, qualiter unusquisque ad palmam martyrii venerit tantummodo explicemus. Beatissima Zoe in Apostolorum natale dum ad Confessionem Petri apostoli oraret, ab insidiantibus paganis arctatur, duciturque ad patronum regionis Naumachiae, et compellitur Martis statunculo, quod illic stabat, thuris guttas incendere. Tum illa respondit: Mulierem Marti sacrificare compellitis, ut ostendatis Martem vestrum mulieribus delectari. Sed ille impudicissimae Veneri potuit pudorem eripere, mihi vero tropaeum fidei in fronte portanti non poterit praevalere. Non enim ego meis contra eum viribus luctor; sed in Domini mei Jesu Christi virtute confidens, et vos et illum pariter ridendo contemno. Tunc patronus regionis

misit eam in custodiam obscurissimam, et per quinque dies fecit eam nec lumen videre, nec cibum nec potum accipere. Solum vox ejus qui eam illic incluserat audiebatur dicentis: Ibi morieris fame, et siti, et caecitate, nisi te libaturam repromiseris diis.

74. Sed cum pertransissent sex dies suggesserunt de ea praefecto saevienti: qui jussit eam a collo et capillis in arborem excelsam suspendi et subter fumum ex sterquilinio adhiberi. Statim autem ut suspensa est, in confessione Domini emisit spiritum. Illi autem auferentes corpus ejus saxo ligaverunt et Tiberis alveo immerserunt, dicentes: Ne Christiani corpus ejus tollant, et faciant sibi illam deam.

75. Igitur celebrato martyrio ejus, venit in somnis B. Sebastiano, et narravit ei qualiter martyrium Domini suscepisset. Quod cum narrasset S. Sebastianus, proripuit se S. Tranquillinus, dicens: Feminae ad coronam praecedunt, ut quid vivimus? Ipse quoque descendens Apostolorum natalitii octavo die, ad B. Pauli Confessionem accessit: nihilominus et ipse perpessus insidias tentus est, et a populo lapidatus mortuus est, et corpus ejus Tiberino gurgiti mancipatum est.

76. Item Nicostratus et Claudius una cum Castorio et Victorino et Symphoriano, dum corpora Sanctorum per ora Tiberina requirerent, a persecutoribus tenti sunt, et ad Urbis praefectum perducti. Erat judex Fabianus, qui eos hortabatur ad sacrificandum, et per decem dies minis eos et blanditiis agens in nullo penitus potuit commovere. Tunc fecit de iis suggestionem imperatoribus, qui jusserunt eos usque tertio torqueri. Cumque nulla ratione tormentis compulsi cederent, jussit eos in medio mari praecipites dari. Immensis igitur arctati ponderibus, pelagi fluctibus dati sunt, et in loco mundo inter aquas coronam martyrii celebrarunt. Insidiabantur itaque

infideles fidelibus, et iniquo furore vexati christianum non poterant nec nomen audire.

CAPUT XXI. S. Tiburtii martyrium.

77. Interea dum S. Caio episcopo quidam se simulata fide sociasset, dicens se esse Christianum; porro hic apostata exstiterat et erat fraudulentus in omni sermone, et callidus in omni commisso. Quid multa? dum a B. Tiburtio viro scholasticissimo et nobili et sancto frequenter argueretur, quod capillos super apicem frontis tonsoris arte componeret, et quod assidue pasceretur et ludendo pranderet; et quod licentius feminarum se aspectibus daret, et quod a jejuniis se et orationibus tolleret, quod somno deditus non interesset pervigil in hymnis Dei ducentibus noctes; dum pro his, ut diximus, a B. Tiburtio acrius argueretur, simulat se aequanimiter monentem accipere: et egit arte quatenus orantem S. Tiburtium comprehenderent infideles. In qua comprehensione seipsum teneri fecit, et simul ad secretarium perduci judicis saevientis. At ubi introducti sunt, Fabianus praefectus dixit ad eum, qui se arte tradiderat: Quis diceris? At ille respondit: Torquatus. Fabianus dixit: Quid profiteris? Torquatus dixit: Christianus sum. Fabianus dixit: Ignoras quod jusserunt invictissimi principes, ut qui sacrificare diis noluerint diversis suppliciis macerentur? Torquatus dixit: Hic magister meus est, et ipse me semper docuit: quod hunc videro facere, necesse est ut faciam.

78. Fabianus conversus ad S. Tiburtium dixit: Audisti quid Torquatus asserat? quid ad ista respondes? S. Tiburtius dixit: Torquatus diu est quod se Christianum esse mentitur; virtus enim nominis ipsius sancti graviter fert et moleste, suum nomen non a suis amatoribus usurpari. Revera enim, vir illustrissime, hoc Christianum vocabulum, divinae virtutis est, sectatorum videlicet Christi, qui vere philosophati sunt, qui vere Christiani dicti sunt, qui

ad obterendas libidines fortiter dimicarunt. Credisne, vir illustrissime, hunc esse Christianum, qui in lenocinio sui moliendo capitis fimbrias committit, qui tonsorem diligit, qui scapulas molliter gestit, qui fluxum gressum improbo nisu distendit, qui viros negligenter agit, feminas diligentius intuetur. Numquam tales Christus habere dignatus est servos. Verum quoniam me hic se imitaturum asseruit, hic in tuo conspectu probabis eum esse mentitum. Hic enim qualis semper fuerit nunc evidenter ostendet.

79. Fabianus dixit: Consultius facies, si saluti tuae consulas, et principum decreta non contemnas. S. Tiburtius dixit: Ego saluti meae melius non consulo, quam ut deos deasque contemnas, unum Dominum Jesum Christum Deum meum esse confitear. Torquatus dixit: Non solum ipse Christianus crudelis est, verum etiam multos persuadet, et decipit, ac docet omnes deos daemones esse; ipse autem cum sociis suis, cum quibus magicas artes exercet die noctuque incantationibus occupatur. S. Tiburtius dixit: Falsus testis non erit impunitus. Et ait judici: Iste, quem vides, illustrissime vir, malitiae suae curis exaestuans ad nihil aliud Christianis est junctus, nisi ut cogitaret quomodo se nobis quasi Christianum ostenderet; quomodo aliis se fidelissimum mentiretur. Reprehendebam tamen in eo Cyclopeam edacitatem, et mersum vino pudorem, et sepultam divini nominis sanctitatem. Ebrius patiebatur sitim, et esuriem vomens: nec ut Christianus, sed ut Antonianus quoddam ille conviva manducabat, bibebat, vomebat, et nunc Christianos arguit, Christianos accusat, in nos mitem judicem incitat, gladium nolenti judici porrigit, et ut daemoniis cervices nostras inclinemus hortatur. Videmus votum tuum, videmus cruenta consilia; et scelerata arte verborum venena tui pectoris intuemur. Accingere nunc crudelissime: utere carnificis officio: vendica tibi et ipsius judicis vocem; applica aculeos, suspende Christianos, damna, percute, incende, universa tormenta adhibe, bene nos accepisti. Si exsilium minaris, hoc philosophantibus totus est mundus; si supplicium, evadimus mundi carcerem;

si ignes, majora horum in cupiditatibus vincimus. Decerne quidquid libet, omnis nobis vilis est poena ubi pura comes est conscientia.

80. Fabianus praefectus dixit: Restitue te generi tuo, et hoc esto quod te natura dictavit. Nobilis enim natus ad tantam devolutus es faecem, ut velis et supplicium simul et infamiam subire et mortem. S. Tiburtius dixit: O prudentissimum virorum, et Romanis judicem constitutum! quia meretricem Venerem, et incestum Jovem, et Mercurium fallacem, et Saturnum filiorum occisorem colere nolo, infamiam generositatis incurro: et quia unum et verum Deum, qui in coelis regnat, adoro et veneror, suppliciis me macerandum esse minaris. Non annuimus tuae persuasioni: non negamus; Christum Filium Dei ad hoc de coelo descendisse ad terras, ut a terris homo ad coelum posset ascendere; ideo istas omnes vanas effigies, quas colitis sine causa, proculcans pedibus meis, Deo me omnipotenti subjeci.

81. Tunc Fabianus jussit ante pedes ejus carbones ardentes effundi; et ait ad eum: Elige tibi unum e duobus, aut thura in istis carbonibus adjice, aut pedibus super eos nudis incede. Tunc B. Tiburtius faciens signum crucis, constanter nuda super eos ingressus est planta, et coepit praefecto dicere: Depone infidelitatem et disce quia hic solus est Deus, quem confitemur creaturis omnibus dominari. Mitte tu, si potes, in nomine Jovis dei tui manus in calidam aquam; et si potest Jovis tuus, faciat te non sentire fervorem ardoris. Nam mihi in nomine Domini mei Jesu Christi videtur, quod super roseos flores gradior, quia creatura Creatoris sui famulatur imperio.

82. Fabianus dixit: Quis ignorat magicam vos docuisse Christum vestrum? S. Tiburtius dixit: Obmutesce, infelix, et noli auribus meis hanc injuriam facere, ut audiam te rabido ore latrantem, mellifluum nomen ejus sanctum nominare. Tunc iratus Fabianus dictavit sententiam dicens: Blasphemator deórum, et reus

atrocium injuriarum, gladio animadvertatur. Ductus est autem via Lavicana tertio milliario ab Urbe, et effundens orationem ad Dominum uno ictu gladii verberatus abscessit. Et in eodem loco a parente quodam Christiano sepultus est: in quo loco multa beneficia semper praestitit Christus ad laudem nominis sui usque in praesentem diem.

CAPUT XXII. SS. Castuli, Marcelliani, Marci, caedes.

83. Post haec autem Torquatus egit ut Castulus zetarius palatii, hospes Sanctorum, comprehenderetur: qui cum fuisset arctatus, et hic tertio appensus, tertio auditus, in confessione Domini perseverans, missus est in foveam et dimissa est super eum massa arenaria, et ipse cum palma martyrii migravit ad Dominum.

84. Tenentur post haec Marcellianus et Marcus; et ambo ligati ad stipitem clavos in pedibus acutos acceperunt; quibus dicebat insanissimus Fabianus: Tamdiu fixis stabitis plantis, quousque diis debitum redhibeatis officium. Tunc ambo fratres in uno ligno confixi psallebant dicentes: Ecce quam bonum et quam jucundum habitare fratres in unum. Dicit eis Fabianus: Infelices et miseri, deponite amentiam vestram, et liberate vosmetipsos a cruciatibus imminentibus super vos. Cui respondentes ambo dixerunt: Numquam tam bene epulati sumus: modo coepimus esse fixi in amore Christi. Utinam nos sic esse sicut sumus tamdiu permittas, quamdiu hujus tegimur corporis indumento. Cumque transisset una dies et una nox, et illi in psalmis et hymnis perseverarent, jussit eos ambos ubi stabant lanceis per latera verberari: et ita per martyrii gloriam ad siderea regna migraverunt. Item sepulti sunt et ipsi in via Appia, milliario secundo ab Urbe, in loco qui vocatur Ad Arenas, quia cryptae arenarum illic erant, ex quibus Urbis moenia struebantur.

CAPUT XXIII. S. Sebastiani gloriosum certamen.

85. His ita gestis B. Sebastianus ab insidiantibus conventus est: et quia, ut diximus, videbatur sub chlamyde latere, cum miles esset dignissimus Christi, suggessit de eo praefectus Diocletiano imperatori. Quem Diocletianus ad se convocans, ait: Ego te inter primos palatii mei semper habui. Et tu contra salutem meam in injuriam deorum hactenus latuisti. S. Sebastianus dixit: Pro salute ua semper Christum colui, et pro statu Romani orbis illum, qui in coelis est, semper adoravi, considerans a lapidibus auxilium petere insani capitis esse et vani. Tunc iratus Diocletianus jussit eum duci in medium campum, et ligari quasi signum ad sagittam, et jussit ut sagittarii eum figerent. Tunc posuerunt eum milites in medio campo et hinc inde eum ita sagittis repleverunt, ut quasi hericius ita esset hirsutus ictibus sagittarum.

86. Aestimantes autem illum esse mortuum abierunt. Tunc relicta martyris Castuli zetarii, nomine Irene, abiit nocte, ut corpus ejus tolleret et sepeliret. Et inveniens eum viventem adduxit ad domum suam in scala excelsa ubi manebat ad palatium, et ibi intra paucos dies salutem integerrimam recuperavit in omnibus membris.

87. Cumque omnes Christiani ad eum convenirent, hortabantur eum abscedere. Ille autem oratione facta descendit, et stans super gradus Heliogabali, venientibus imperatoribus dixit: Iniquis subreptionibus animos imperii vestri templorum pontifices obsident, suggerentes de Christianis falsa commenta, dicentes eos Reipubl. esse adversarios; quorum orationibus ipsa Respublica melioratur, et crescit; qui pro imperio vestro et pro salute Romani exercitus orare non cessant. Cum haec et talia diceret, Diocletianus ait: Tune es Sebastianus, quem nos dudum sagittis jusseramus interfici? S. Sebastianus dixit: Ad hoc me Dominus meus Jesus Christus resuscitare dignatus est, ut

conveniam et contester vos coram omni populo, injusto judicio persecutionem vestram in Christi famulos ebullisse.

88. Tunc jussit eum in hippodromo palatii duci, et tam diu fustigari, quamdiu spiritum exhalaret. Tunc tulerunt corpus ejus nocte, et in cloacam Maximam miserunt dicentes: ne forte Christiani eum sibi martyrem faciant. Tunc B. Sebastianus apparuit in somnis S. Lucinae cuidam matronae religiosissimae dicens: In cloaca illa, quae est juxta circum, invenies corpus meum pendens in gompho. Hoc tu dum levaveris perduces ad catacumbas et sepelies in initio cryptae juxta vestigia Apostolorum.

89. Tunc B. Lucina ipsa per se cum servis suis medio noctis abiit, et levans eum posuit in pavone suo, et perduxit ad locum, ubi ipse imperaverat, et cum omni diligentia sepelivit. Ipsa autem sancta Lucina per XXX dies a loco sancto ipso non discessit.

90. Post aliquantos autem annos pax Ecclesiae est reddita: quae statim ut Ecclesia gloriam pacis accepit, domum suam fecit ecclesiam. Cui omnes suas opes ad Christianorum requiem relinquens, fecit ipsam Ecclesiam haeredem in Christo, qui cum Deo Patre et Spiritu sancto aequalis vivit et regnat in unitate virtutis in saecula saeculorum. Amen.

The Scriptorium Project is the work of a small group of lay people of various apostolic churches who are interested in the preservation, transmission, and translation of the works of the early and medieval church. Our efforts are to make the works of the church fathers accessible to anyone who might have an interest in Christian antiquities and the theological, philosophical, and moral writings that have become the bedrock of Western Civilization.

To-date, our releases have pulled from the Greek, Syriac, Georgian, Latin, Celtic, Ethiopian, and Coptic traditions of Christianity, and have been pulled from sundry local traditions and languages.

www.ingramcontent.com/pod-product-compliance
Ingram Content Group UK Ltd.
Pitfield, Milton Keynes, MK11 3LW, UK
UKHW020428070325
455838UK00014B/492